The Real Diana Dors

The Real Diana Dors

Anna Cale

WHITE OWL

AN IMPRINT OF PEN & SWORD BOOKS LTD.
YORKSHIRE – PHILADELPHIA

First published in Great Britain in 2021 by
Pen & Sword White Owl
An imprint of
Pen & Sword Books Ltd
Yorkshire – Philadelphia

ISBN 978 1 52678 215 1

Typeset by Mac Style
Printed and bound in Great Britain by
CPI Group (UK) Ltd, Croydon, CR0 4YY

Pen & Sword Books Limited incorporates the imprints of Atlas,
Archaeology, Aviation, Discovery, Family History, Fiction, History,
Maritime, Military, Military Classics, Politics, Select, Transport,
True Crime, Air World, Frontline Publishing, Leo Cooper, Remember
When, Seaforth Publishing, The Praetorian Press, Wharncliffe
Local History, Wharncliffe Transport, Wharncliffe True Crime
and White Owl.

For a complete list of Pen & Sword titles please contact

PEN & SWORD BOOKS LIMITED
47 Church Street, Barnsley, South Yorkshire, S70 2AS, England
E-mail: enquiries@pen-and-sword.co.uk
Website: www.pen-and-sword.co.uk

Or

PEN AND SWORD BOOKS
1950 Lawrence Rd, Havertown, PA 19083, USA
E-mail: Uspen-and-sword@casematepublishers.com
Website: www.penandswordbooks.com

Contents

Acknowledgements

I am incredibly grateful for the support and encouragement of many people during the process of writing this book. But special thanks go to the following: Barrie Rutter for sharing his time so generously; and Gemma Ramsay, Abi Saffrey, Amanda Lynch and Odette Illingworth for their practical and emotional support. I would like to thank fellow writers Chris Nickson, Richard Smyth, James Clarke, James Oddy, Lee Broughton, Michael Brooke, Simon Brew, Tony Hannan, John Leman Riley, and especially Melanie Williams, for their helpful advice and guidance. Thanks also to Jack Simpson and Henry Weekes from the Hyde Park Book Club for taking the time to assist me with research.

I am thankful for the support of my family and friends, but very special thanks to my husband Alan and our daughter Daisy for their patience and understanding, and for welcoming Diana Dors into our lives for so long.

Prologue:
Why Diana Dors is a Lasting Screen Icon

Diana Dors was a uniquely British film star. Few performers have captured the hearts and imaginations of the public in the way Diana did. More than thirty-five years after her premature death in 1984 aged just 52, she remains a familiar face, entering the public consciousness and symbolising to many fans a bygone age of glamour. She was an ordinary girl from Swindon who became seen as Britain's answer to Marilyn Monroe.

But Diana was a star in her own right, and hers is a story of determination, personal struggle and setbacks on the road to fame. Her private life was a rollercoaster. As well as the highs of screen stardom, she also endured tragedy, illness, and personal disappointment. She married three times and had a string of love affairs and heartbreaks, but was also the proud mother of three sons. She found herself in court on more than one occasion, was declared bankrupt, accused of obscenity, and had her private life debated in parliament and in public.

Many remember her as an outspoken and sometimes controversial figure, grabbing headlines for her personal life as often as her film roles. She lived her life through the glare of publicity, but she ushered in a new kind of stardom through her relationship with the press and how she used the medium to drive interest in her career. For Diana, image seemed to be everything, but there was more to her than the 'blonde bombshell' reputation suggested. A talented actress, she worked on numerous film and television projects with influential directors, building a fascinating career that spanned decades.

Her acting career began in the shadow of the Second World War, entering the film world as a vulnerable young teenager and negotiating the difficult British studio system of the 1940s and 1950s, where careers for young stars were often brief. Yet she battled against the odds to become one of the most iconic British performers of the twentieth century.

Often, her film roles exploited her looks more than they did her acting talent, and she found herself typecast as the bad girl or the femme fatale. She was the girl who was 'troubled' or about to make some for everyone else. Sometimes she suffered at the hands of directors who were keen to exploit her expendable image. 'I have been strangled, poisoned, hanged, and gassed on movies and TV,' she joked to one journalist in 1963.

But she was always popular with the British public, who developed a fondness for her. Seemingly honest and not afraid to speak her mind, her 'no holds barred' approach to life was fascinating for audiences, and a gift for newspaper editors.

As an actress she seemed to have a unique understanding of what the camera wanted, and what audiences wanted to see from her. But her screen career was often patchy and unpredictable. She experienced critical success for her performance in *Yield to the Night* in 1956, but also faced disappointment when the phone stopped ringing and her private life gained more attention than her acting in the 1960s and 1970s. Her ambitions for international fame were dented by bad luck and poor decisions, but she was not afraid to still take risks, both professionally and personally, over the course of her life.

Diana's personal story has been replayed in the press over the years, often as a fall from grace. The interest in the tragedies she endured, and the men she married, frequently outweighed any focus on her career. Some feel she perhaps became a parody of herself. She is seen as an image rather than a whole person, a snapshot of blonde hair and pouting lips, becoming brassier over time. The blame for her lack of sustained success and happiness is laid firmly at her feet. But she was a complex woman, more than just a sex symbol who craved fame and fortune at any cost. She lived through a period of large social upheaval and changing expectations for women.

In recent years there has been interest in her legacy as a performer, a renewed focus on her as a woman who achieved success in her own right, challenged expectations and changed the way we perceive fame. She was a chameleon who went from being 'Britain's number one bad girl' in the

1950s to a familiar staple of British prime time television by the 1980s, adding a touch of kitsch glamour wherever she went.

Set against the backdrop of the changing social landscape of twentieth-century Britain, this book charts the ups and downs of her diverse acting career and her tumultuous private life, to build a fascinating picture of the 'real' Diana Dors; a truly unique British screen icon.

Chapter 1

The Road to LAMDA

From a young age Diana Dors dreamed of screen stardom, and of parties at glamorous Hollywood houses with swimming pools. She was destined to make a splash. She certainly made an entrance.

Diana Mary Fluck was born in Swindon on 23 October 1931, the only child of Albert Fluck and his wife Mary. Mary's pregnancy was risky due to her advanced age. She had a difficult labour which lasted almost a week, and when Diana finally arrived, she was almost black, leading the doctors to believe that Mary had miscarried. Her own life in the balance, Mary was attended to and Diana swiftly taken away to be revived. A dramatic start to a dramatic life.

Bert and Mary Fluck were a complex couple. They had met in Swindon during the First World War. Bert was Swindon born and raised. Mary was born in Wales but had moved to Swindon with her first husband, William Padget, shortly before the war. When war broke out, William had enlisted but was killed in action, leaving poor young Mary a war widow in an unfamiliar town, away from her own family. She sought work, and became one of the country's first postwomen, a role she took great pride in. She threw herself into her job, and eventually fate intervened when she met the handsome, young, local man who would become her second husband.

A wartime courtship was not easy, but it led to marriage, and the couple tied the knot on 9 March 1918. It was hardly a romantic time; they spent their honeymoon at Osborne House, an army convalescence home on the Isle of Wight, where Bert was sent to recover from war injuries. As an officer with the Royal Warwickshire Regiment, Bert was stationed for a time in India. He had a charm about him and was always popular at dances – he was a good dancer and liked a waltz. But his time in India led to ill health which plagued him in his later years, including a heart condition that was a lasting legacy of contracting malaria. He was also injured after being shelled in France, receiving a nasty eye injury which almost blinded him. The army sent him home, with word that he would probably only have another ten years to live. This put paid to his dancing and his football playing, and likely led to his dissatisfaction in middle age, with such a burden hanging over him and the family. As it was, he outlived his wife by a number of years in the end.

After the war, Mary and Bert settled into a normal domestic life together. Bert found a job on the railways working as a clerk. He steadily worked his way up, eventually becoming Second in Command of the Statistical Section Regional Accounts Department. It seemed a solid and unspectacular middle-class marriage on the face of things, eventually resulting in the arrival of baby Diana thirteen years later, when Bert was 38 and Mary was 42. A surprise addition, but a family at last.

Bert and Mary were a popular couple and their early married life was largely pleasant. Bert excelled at the piano, despite his mother disposing of the family piano after his father's death when he was young. He had indulged in his beloved piano-playing again whilst convalescing from his war injuries previously, and Mary had a good singing voice. They were often invited to perform at social functions.

As time went on, Bert led a full and active life outside the marital home, despite his health concerns and perhaps making up for them. He had a busy social life, playing piano at the Swindon Empire and helping out at the Working Men's Club. Mary hardly saw him, and he certainly was not there when she went into labour with their baby at the Haven Nursing Home just yards from their home in Marlborough Road. Instead, he was giving a speech at the local Masonic Lodge where he had recently become Worshipful Master.

Mary Fluck doted on her precious daughter, Diana. After all, it had been a near miraculous birth, with the newborn practically given up for dead, and Mary had almost lost her own life in the process. Such a journey created an unyielding bond between mother and daughter, one which Mary's husband jealously resented as all her time and affection was now directed to the infant instead of him. A new baby created havoc in Bert's normally ordered existence and put paid to the couple's house parties. Instead, he focused on his life outside the family home, leaving Mary to look after Diana, a situation Mary resented in the longer term. But there was help at hand from Mary's sister, Diana's Aunty Kit, whom Diana adored.

Diana always felt closer to her mother, which is perhaps not surprising given her father's seemingly cold and distant persona, and there was possibly a hint of jealousy of his wife's deep affection for her only child. Yet there was a suggestion of frustration for Mary too, particularly as Bert just carried on as normal and left her to do all the work at home. The parties at home had to stop but it did not alter his life at all. Diana recalled in her 1981 autobiography, *Dors by Diana*, 'Later in life, in moments of anger, my mother would complain how I had completely changed her life, reminding me of the sacrifices she'd had to make as a result of having me.'

Diana described her mother as a beautiful woman with dark blue eyes and long, dark hair that she could sit on, which her father adored. 'When my mother cut her hair in the twenties' bob fashion, he did not speak to her for three weeks,' Diana said, recalling her father's rather Victorian attitudes.

For some years, the couple had been great friends with a man named Gerry Lack. They were a constant threesome, taking holidays together, purchasing a shared car, socialising, and throwing parties. Bert was often out with his own friends, leaving Mary in the dependable company of their friend Gerry. In later years, Diana herself hinted that there was perhaps more to her mother's relationship than friendship, that 'Uncle Gerry' was ever-present for a reason. Diana later thought her father ridiculously naïve not to have suspected anything, or incredibly selfish, perhaps regarding it as a great relief to pass the baton to Gerry from time to time.

Ironically, Gerry Lack was asked to be Diana's godparent, along with her Aunty Kit and Aunty Gwen. It was soon after this occasion that Lack disappeared from their lives, Mary apparently suspecting him of philandering instead of remaining loyal to their friendship. Without Lack's presence in her life, Mary focused on devoting herself to the infant Diana: 'Having presumably got over this man, and with my father out most of the time, my mother allowed her obsession for me to become stronger than ever.' However, Diana never found out the truth about her mother's relationship with Lack.

Previous generations of Diana's family had lived a simple rural life, but the Flucks now enjoyed a very middle-class existence. Diana referred to the feeling of continual torment of forever wondering 'What would the neighbours think?' that dominated her childhood in Swindon. They lived in a smart, modern, semi-detached house on Marlborough Road in the Old Town, an affluent area, and her parents seemed to fit in perfectly. She strongly felt her later aversion to that particular class of people resulted from her parents' 'Snobbish, respectable, bourgeois lifestyle; of being the only daughter of an ex-Army captain living in a hypocritical, narrow-minded community.'

Diana's wider family was sprawling, with so many relatives they were hard to count. She remembered her encounters with her 'Grandma with the teapots', Catherine Fluck, her father's mother. There were compulsory Sunday visits which she was practically dragged along to as a young child. Her Aunty Gwen, her father's sister, the epitome of Victorian values and misery, was usually there too. As Diana recounts in her 1981 autobiography, 'Those boring, dreary Sunday evening teas gave birth to my loathing of Sunday, with its closed shops and everyone sitting around, doing nothing interesting within the sound of church bells.'

Diana's maternal grandmother was quite a different prospect. She affectionately called her 'Grandma with the chick-chicks', on account of the chickens she kept at her remote little pink-washed cottage in Wales that Diana visited for holidays as a young child. It was a very happy time for the young girl, with memories of running through hayfields in the summer. She fondly remembered her other Welsh relatives, her mother being from a large family with seven brothers and one sister. Apart from one uncle who had sadly died in the First World War, they all lived nearby. As an only child, Diana embraced the experience of a large, loving family.

Diana felt an affinity with her Grandma Dors and it is no coincidence that she chose her name when fame beckoned. Georgina Dors had married a young farmer at 16 and soon had children, including Diana's mother Mary, settling into rural life in Somerset. But she met and fell in love with the handsome brother of her husband. She and her brother-in-law, James Payne, ran away together, heading for the Welsh border, and taking Georgina's young children with them. Her husband gave chase on his horse but failed to locate the lovers as they fled into Wales to be together.

Forever ostracised from the family and her friends, Georgina lived unmarried with James, with no money or permanent work between them. Poverty-stricken, they had a further six children together. This was a theme that was to dominate Diana's own life and perhaps be her downfall: her pursuit of love against the odds. Diana said later, 'Grandma let her heart rule her head where men were concerned and was, like me, a perfect target for Cupid's arrows when a dark-eyed man appeared.'

When she reached her teens, Diana's mother Mary moved out of the family home in the Welsh Borders and became a lady's maid at a nearby manor house. It was there she met her first husband, William Padget, who worked as a groom. Perhaps recollecting the comments from her mother or grandmother, Diana described William as 'a ne'er-do-well with a passion for gambling', but Mary married him anyway, perhaps to escape from her humdrum life and circumstances, and the fact she really did not get on with her stepfather, James. Mary was possibly demonstrating the questionable judgement where men were concerned that Diana herself showed throughout her life.

Mary's older brother had become engaged to a local girl before going to fight in France, and he asked his mother to look out for her while he was gone. Unfortunately, stepfather James still had a keen eye for a pretty girl and he and the young woman disappeared together, deserting Georgina and leaving her heartbroken. Yet despite this, James remained the love of Georgina's life and when he died years later, she demanded that her sons attend the funeral and pay their respects.

Diana herself enjoyed a comfortable childhood. Nothing was too much for the young Miss Fluck. She was perhaps the best-dressed young child in the neighbourhood, and she wanted for nothing. Each birthday was celebrated with a lavish party, and dance classes were a must. She enjoyed frequent trips to the cinema, which fuelled a love of films for Diana: 'Sitting there in the dark with my mother, we were transported to a world far away from Swindon; to glamorous Hollywood homes and nightclubs where people wore beautiful clothes, swam in luxurious pools, and sang, danced or acted their way across lavish sets.'

By the time it came to starting school, Mary felt only the best was good enough for her precious daughter. Diana was sent, at great expense and against her father's wishes, to a small private school run by two prim sisters, Miss Daisy and Miss Ruth. Selwood House School should have been the making of her, yet Diana spent her time daydreaming in class instead of focusing on her lessons. She scribbled film star names on her paper instead of sums. Her school reports were disappointing, which enraged her father and led to another round of him despairing of his hopeless daughter. Her more pragmatic mother simply responded that as long as she could add up her weekly wage, that was all Diana needed to know.

Diana later recalled one particular English lesson where the children were asked to write an essay on what they would like to be when they were grown up. The young, yet already ambitious, Diana wrote that she 'Was going to be a film star, with a cream telephone and a swimming pool.' She was already dreaming of being a star, and apparently had no doubt in her mind that it would happen.

Bert had always wanted his daughter to take up the piano like him. Twice he tried to teach her himself unsuccessfully and once he sent her to a tutor, but she was not gifted like him and failed to practise. Bert was very disappointed in Diana, threatening to 'wash his hands of her'. Such talk would unfortunately become a recurring theme in their troubled relationship. Remarking later on her father, Diana felt there was nothing of her he approved of and yet acknowledged that it must have been hard for him to raise an only girl: 'I do feel guilty about those early days and realise he wanted only what was best for a girl child. I came to understand, when it was all too late, that whereas one can rebel against a father, mother or husband, one cannot do so against one's own children.'

This difficult relationship with her father perhaps set the tone for her own romantic life in later years. She struggled to understand him and his feelings, his motives and his ideals. Yet she also felt the emotional barriers between them, possibly created by the doubt about him being her natural father. It left Diana feeling confused and it ate away at their relationship. She often felt he resented her being there at all. Other male figures in her life, and in her family's past, would also play on her mind. Her

'Uncle' Gerry, who despite being ever-present and doting on Mary, soon disappeared from the scene when baby Diana came along. Her Grandma Georgina's beloved James had his head turned by a pretty young girl and deserted her. The pursuit of love and pleasure, and the ramifications of following one's heart, would play heavily in Diana's life.

Even at a young age, Diana was already showing a keen interest in the opposite sex, and the path of young love did not exactly run smooth from the outset. The first boy she spotted in the playground decided to punch her in the eye, giving her a nasty shock and a terrible shiner. Afterwards, this led to terrible eye problems that plagued her childhood, and a lazy eye for which she needed to wear an eyepatch. Her eyesight never fully recovered, even in adulthood. By her own admission, she vainly discarded her glasses at every opportunity in case a man should see her in them!

Despite her unfortunate first encounter with a boy, she soon transferred her affections to another one and they immediately became sweethearts, announcing their intention to marry at the first opportunity. Yet he disappeared from her affections after her birthday party, as she apparently did not like the china tea-set he gave her as a present. This was to be a pattern that Diana followed a number of times through the years.

Mary continued to cater to Diana's needs and whims. She took her to have her straight hair permed, much to the annoyance of Bert. His angry retorts and finger-wagging at both of them only served to strengthen the bond between mother and daughter, united further in their rebellion, as thick as thieves. Sometimes Mary would give in to Diana's pleas not to go to school, and they would sneak off for afternoon trips to the cinema. Like many women of her generation, for Mary, the movies were an escape from her unfulfilling life; her own dreams of being a singer had been cut short by marriage and responsibility. As Diana recounts, 'Off we'd romp, hand in hand, and for a couple of magical hours watch our film star idols before rushing home to have my father's tea ready on the table when he returned from the office.'

Mary was determined that Diana should not speak with a broad Swindon accent, so she persuaded Bert to let her have elocution lessons. Diana enjoyed these and excelled at them. Her elocution mistress entered her for various prizes and medals, which she happily won. Diana also gained some local recognition and she loved to see her own photo in the local paper. Still bored at school, Diana dreamed of the life she could have when she grew up; waiting for it to happen felt like an eternity to her and she longed to escape from her seemingly dreary existence. Books and her much-loved trips to the cinema were her only solace.

Life in the Fluck household continued to be tricky to navigate for young Diana as tensions often surfaced. It was hardly a life of domestic bliss behind closed doors. When she was around 7 years old, Diana discovered that her mother had been married before, and in light of her own father's behaviour, her vivid imagination conjured up quite a dramatic backstory for her mother's first doomed romance. Her father wanted Diana to get a good job after she left school, perhaps as a secretary, and to meet a decent chap and settle down into marriage and family life. Not an unusual opinion for the times of course, but completely at odds with Diana's dreams for something quite different.

A short time after, thoughts of a bright future were overshadowed by the outbreak of war. It was 1939 and, although 8-year-old Diana knew the gravity of the situation, she also found the drama of it all rather exciting. She felt that anything was preferable to dull old Swindon, and to her it felt like war might liven things up a bit. It was evidence perhaps of Diana's comfortable, sheltered existence, that she failed to acknowledge the true impact the war would have.

As the war continued, concerts were frequently staged at local army bases, and Diana's father was happy to do his bit to entertain the troops, organising shows and providing musical accompaniment on stage with his piano-playing. It was during this time that Diana had her first taste of showbusiness. If a performer could not make it, she would be sent up on stage wearing her red tap shoes and a big smile on her face. The feeling of excitement, the butterflies in her stomach and her heart beating faster was like medicine, and she eagerly awaited every chance to shine on stage. Her limited repertoire of songs and her cute dancing were always received to rapturous applause. This delighted her and fuelled her belief that she was bound to become a big star.

By her own admission, Diana was obsessed with becoming a film star. She fantasised about Hollywood swimming pools, contriving all sorts of exotic scenarios. She was just waiting to be discovered, feeling it was only a matter of time before Hollywood came calling. She had read in her film magazines about stars who were discovered in unusual places, such as Lana Turner being spotted sipping an ice-cream soda in a drugstore, and this gave her ideas. She left notes in dustbins with her address on, thinking that somehow these would be found and magically passed on to Hollywood producers looking for the next Shirley Temple. She was sorely disappointed. Her schoolwork suffered, of course, as she remarked in her first autobiography, *Swingin' Dors*, in 1960, she was distracted, 'Thinking about all the things I was simply aching to do and yet unable to achieve because of a trifling matter like getting an education.'

In the summer of 1943, Diana fell in love for the first time. She might have only been 11 years old, but to her it was absolutely the real thing. Michael was a local boy and they had known each other for years, but that summer, they spent every possible moment together, with secret meetings between them in meadows, discussing their hopes and dreams, and gazing into each other's eyes. Sadly, it was not to last, a fickle Diana turning her back on poor, young Michael after he wore shorts to her birthday party when all the other boys wore long trousers. Her reaction left him bewildered and heartbroken.

As 1944 dawned, there was excitement on the horizon for Hollywood-obsessed Diana – real Americans arrived in town! The local army base could not house them all, so anyone with a spare room was asked to house a GI or two. Being quite affluent, the Flucks indeed had a spare room, much to the delight of Diana. And low and behold, as if it were fate, their GI was from California. However, he was hardly a Hollywood insider as his family owned an orange farm, but he patiently and gallantly answered her myriad of questions about the film stars of the day. Each American she met delighted her with their mannerisms, smoking cigarettes like Humphrey Bogart, chewing gum and spending the money their British counterparts did not have.

At 12 and a half, Diana looked old for her age and had taken to wearing make-up when her father was not looking. Her honey-coloured hair was long and she wore it as fancy as she could. Walking about the town, GIs would jokingly shout that she looked like Veronica Lake. The attention was a gift to her. Walking home from the cinema one evening with her mother, they encountered a large group of GIs, who begged them to come along to a dance at a local hotel. Diana was thrilled and although her mother hesitated, she soon gave in. It was like a dream for Diana. They rushed home and she changed into her best red dress, put on a pair of real nylons and high heels, her hair done in as glamorous a style as a girl from Swindon could manage. Like Cinderella, she was on her way to the ball.

She danced all night, a whirlwind of GIs with their compliments and offers of drinks ensuring she was never short of a partner. She felt so grown-up that when asked her age, she cheekily said 17, finally living out the dreams of an older version of herself: 'My head was a-whirl with sweet nothings and compliments whispered in my ear, and although I drank only Coca Cola, it might as well have been champagne.' It was some enchanted evening.

Diana begged her mother to let her attend the local dance hall every Saturday night, with her as chaperone. It felt like she was living a double life. Each weekday she attended school, a 13-year-old schoolgirl in her uniform, but on Saturday nights, she transformed herself into a glamorous dance hall star, the fawning GIs none the wiser. It was ironic that she would later find fame with the film *Dance Hall* in 1950, playing a character not unlike her teenage self. Life was a happy, carefree whirl of dancing dates and parties, all the teenage Diana could wish for. Soon the war ended and the Americans returned home. But it made Diana all the more determined to go to America herself and follow her dream of becoming a film star.

After her experience of dancing with the American boys, the local schoolboys just did not cut it any more. But Diana still gave them a chance, organising mini dance parties of her own so she could impress them with her jitterbug. There was teenage smooching, but she missed the thrill of the American dance hall parties. There were some familiar faces amongst her teenage admirers, one being the boy who had given her the black eye all those years before, although he was more interested in kissing than teasing her now.

It was during this time that Diana struck up a friendship with Desmond Morris. He was a local lad, a bit older than Diana, and his mum ran a tobacconist's shop nearby. Being older, having reached the grand age of 17, meant he also had a car. Diana, Desmond and other friends would take road trips into the countryside, and enjoy a bit of fresh air and teenage kissing. They kept in touch over the years, exchanging letters when Diana moved to London. She even sent him a handful of pin-up shots on request when Morris was in the army, which made him rather popular with his fellow soldiers.

Morris went on to become a successful zoologist, broadcaster and writer on human biology, amongst other subjects. When they were reunited on the *Parkinson* talk show many years later in 1971, Diana quipped that the last time they'd seen each other, they were necking in the back of his car, 'He was not man-watching in those days, he was girl-watching.' Morris also became a Surrealist artist and produced a painting of Diana in 1946 called *Girl Selling Flowers* based on their teenage love affair, which now hangs in Swindon's art gallery. His work was exhibited with that of Joan Miró in an exhibition in 1948, and he went on to become a prolific artist in his own right. But he would always be Diana's 'teenage crush' whom she taught to jitterbug in his grandma's back garden in Swindon.

Still aged in her early teens, in a set-up that would be echoed in one of her early films, *Lady Godiva Rides Again* (1951), on the annual family holiday to Weston-Super-Mare, Diana entered a local beauty contest to find a pin-up girl for *Soldier* magazine. Once again, she gave her age as 17 and looked every inch of it as she strutted her stuff around the lido for the judges, wearing a scarlet and white swimsuit and channelling her inner Betty Grable as best she could. To her amazement, she came third. But as this meant she appeared in the local Swindon newspaper, her exploits cemented her reputation as a bit of a bad girl. However, the exposure led to an offer of work as a photographic model for a local art professor at the American college, clothed in a swimsuit, of course. When the professor compared her to some of the glamour girls of the time, she had no idea what he meant but it sounded nice to her.

At barely 14, things were finally happening for the determined Diana. Hearing of her wish to be an actress, she was offered theatre work at the college too. It was not her beloved film, but it was a start. She appeared in productions of *A Weekend in Paris* and *Death Takes a Holiday*, taking the lead role for one week in the latter to good reviews in the campus newspaper. The college acting teacher told her she was a natural who should be in Hollywood. She also sang songs for the college radio station.

This first foray into the world of showbusiness, however small, gave Diana the impetus she needed to finally make a bid for stardom. She was desperate to leave school and managed to persuade her reluctant father to allow her to attend an acting academy in London once a week instead. She was 14 and legally able to leave school (the leaving age was raised to 15 the following year in 1947). He agreed only if she promised she would study for a teaching diploma and return home to Swindon to teach elocution. So off Diana went to study private acting classes at the London Academy of Dramatic Art (LAMDA) each week, with her doting mother at her side.

Diana enjoyed her first trip to a film studio during this time, having been given a letter of introduction to a film producer by the name of Keating through a photographer at the American college. During one of her weekly trips to London, she went to visit the man on set, accompanied by her mother, dressed in her best red coat and excitedly clutching the letter. The film was *This Man is Mine* (1946), a comedy directed by Marcel Varnel and starring Glynis Johns. Being in that environment at last felt like paradise to Diana. She recalled the feeling of standing in the darkness of the studio, 'a pink cloud of ambition floating over her head', staring awestruck at the elaborate detail of the film set, feeling the heat from the dozens of lights, and watching the cast and crew rush about. It turned out that Keating was not actually a producer – he was an assistant director – but he did chat with Diana and put her in touch with a casting director. It was a small but important step, and Diana was in no doubt about her ambition to act. Aged just 14, she was about to take her first steps towards becoming a star.

Chapter 2

A Step Towards Fame

Believing that she would still return home to Swindon and teach elocution rather than follow her fanciful dream to become an actress, and after much insistence from his star-struck daughter, Diana's father reluctantly agreed to let her attend LAMDA full-time instead of one day a week. Her parents were reassured that she would be looked after by the head of the Academy, Wilfred Foulis. They were also satisfied that her day-to-day welfare would be supervised by the lady who ran the Young Women's Christian Association (YWCA) around the corner from the Academy, the delightfully named Miss Whipp.

Diana left Swindon one cold January day in 1946, a suitcase in one hand and a return train ticket in the other. 'It was all very adventurous at the time, but looking back now it seems sad to me when I think about that cold, snowy day,' she recalled. She promised to return home every weekend. On the journey to the station, her father told her that he was letting her have this chance, and she was to work hard but 'failure was unthinkable', a tough thing to hear as a 14-year-old. Diana was excited, but never knew what her parents really thought about the situation. She knew later on that her mother was most likely left broken-hearted by her absence, but supportive of her dreams and the opportunities she had never had. But in that moment, young Diana did not care and the concept of failure just did not enter her mind. She was on her way to London with the chance to make it, and the world would be hers for the taking.

On arrival at the YWCA near Earls Court that was to be her weekday home, Diana handed in her ration book to Miss Whipp and unpacked her things in the room she was to share with three other girls, two of whom were also studying at LAMDA. It was her first ever night away from home.

The next morning Diana was rudely awoken from her slumber by a frighteningly loud bell. Thinking it was the fire alarm, she jumped out of bed, only to discover that it was the waking-up bell and it would sound every morning, rather like in a prison. All the girls had just half an hour to get washed and dressed and downstairs for breakfast.

Diana was to have a stark lesson in budgeting at a young age. Her small allowance from her father was enough to pay for her room, with two meals a day, buy a frugal lunch and leave the remaining few shillings to pay for the underground back to Paddington train station each Friday evening to catch the train home.

Classes at LAMDA started at 10 am each day, and at the age of 14 Diana was the youngest full-time student. There was, however, another young student not much older than her, a boy from Grimsby called George Raestrick, and Diana promptly fell madly in love with him. She recalled in retrospect that he probably looked rather like a young Elvis Presley, with his slicked-back dark hair and amazing green eyes. They immediately made a date for that evening – a trip to the cinema. But as instructed by Miss Whipp, she was home by 10 pm. There would be many evenings in future when Diana would instead sneak in late, shoes in hand, carefully navigating the creaky stairs up to her room on the fifth floor. She was a teenager, after all.

Those first few months at LAMDA went well for Diana, and she soon settled into a routine. Her classes included stage make-up, improvisation, film technique, Shakespeare and the classics, mime and fencing. All the skills an aspiring artist could hope for including, 'Learning such things as how one dies from strychnine poisoning as opposed to arsenic,' she later recalled.

Evenings were spent listening to the radio or on a date with handsome, young George, and weekends started with a train journey home to her parents, her mum always delighted to have her back. By Sunday though, Diana was often reluctant to go back to London after enjoying the comfort and security of home. She felt a sense of disappointment as her time at LAMDA was hardly glamorous. But she knew she had to start somewhere and she was determined to succeed.

It was during this time that Diana found herself an agent. The meeting she had with the casting director earlier in the year was finally paying off, as he was true to his word and did indeed recommend her to an agency. And so, Mr Harbord from the Gordon Harbord Agency got in touch to discuss an upcoming film she might be suitable for.

That film was *Black Narcissus* (1947), the well-respected psychological drama written, produced and directed by the legendary Michael Powell and Emeric Pressburger, and based on the 1939 novel of the same name written by Rumer Godden. The film depicts the ever-growing tensions within a small convent of Anglican nuns on an isolated mountain in the Himalayas, who are there to establish a school and hospital for the local community. It stars Deborah Kerr, Kathleen Byron, Sabu, David Farrar and Flora Robson. Despite Pressburger's reputation for a preference for location shooting, it was filmed predominantly at Pinewood Studios on an elaborate set, with some external shots filmed in Leonardslee Gardens, West Sussex, which was the home of a retired Indian army officer and had appropriate trees and plants for the Indian setting. The set included large landscape paintings as backdrops for the mountains and used intricate and detailed scale models for the building exteriors.

Made in a unique and vibrant colour palette with erotically charged undertones and fascinating performances from the lead actors, particularly the incredibly passionate and wired Byron as Sister Ruth, the film won accolades for its technical mastery and pioneering cinematography from Jack Cardiff. Cardiff went on to win an Academy Award and Golden Globe for his work on the film. Its unusual setting and modernity, and the intricacies of the story, with its eroticism and hint of passion and desire under the surface in such a religious, restricted environment, shocked some audiences. But the film was critically lauded and went on to become very influential for other directors.

At the time of the request to test for the film, Diana hurried to the agent's office in St Martin's Lane, full of excitement at the thought of her first film role. It never occurred to her that she would be required to wear heavy, dark make-up for the role, which was that of an Indian girl.

Black Narcissus was released just a few months before India achieved independence from Britain in August 1947. Only one of the main Indian roles was played by an ethnically Indian actor, Sabu. Other roles were played by white actors in heavy make-up, which was common practice at the time.

Despite her concerns about the character, Diana was delighted to have her first screen test, convinced she was going to be a star. It never crossed her mind that she might not actually get the part. She did not, and the role eventually went to Jean Simmons. As she reflected in 1960, 'In my supreme conceit, at an age when the world is one's oyster, there is no such word as failure…my first lesson in show business heartbreak was learned.'

For Diana, this felt like a massive setback, but she rallied and set about finding her next career opportunity. She found it with the assistance of a photographer at the *Swindon Advertiser*, who helped her secure an evening job as a model for the London Camera Club. It was another lesson in life for Diana to find herself amongst the amateur photographers, who rushed along of an evening to take photos of the scantily clad, often completely nude, young women when their wives were not around. Inevitably, despite her very young age, Diana was asked to remove her swimsuit too. She discussed the proposal with her mother, who consulted her father. Surprisingly, he consented. His reason was that the extra money would be useful and she had already posed nude for life drawing classes anyway, so this was not really that different.

One of the amateur photographers gave her the name of a modelling agency, and again an excited Diana thought this could lead to bigger and better things. She signed up with the Pearl Beresford Agency and waited for the phone to ring.

Her studies at LAMDA were still going well. She had achieved a bronze medal the previous term and was now studying for her silver. She had her first 'modelling' assignment from Pearl Beresford, an uneventful and frankly quite dull time posing for a very serious photographer. But the money was better than the London Camera Club, so Diana stifled her yawns and thought about that instead. The second job was rather more eventful, however. An elderly white-haired man greeted her at the door of the address she had been given. He was a retired naval officer apparently. He kept plying her with unknown drinks, which the naïve young Diana accepted. Her head spinning, she went to undress for the nude photo shoot she was there to undertake. But the session came to an abrupt halt as a ring at the door sent the old man into a spin, and he promptly pushed her into a side room, asking her to dress quickly. A woman's voice suggested to Diana that the man's wife had returned unexpectedly perhaps, and his sordid plans had been thwarted. As he pushed her out of the front door, he gave her £5 to keep quiet. Giddy-headed from the alcohol, Diana returned to her YWCA room for a lie down.

The day would take another dramatic turn, however, as Diana received a very important phone call. It was for her first screen test.

A few days previously, she had sat her silver medal exam at LAMDA and the adjudicator had been a casting director called Eric L'Epine Smith. When he informed her that she had passed with Honours, he also told her that he was casting for a film called *The Shop at Sly Corner*. It was being adapted from the successful stage play by Edward Percy, and he thought she would be perfect for a small part in it. 'My head swam, I was breathless with excitement. What did it matter that it was a small part? Anything would suit me, even a "walk on", just as long as I could get in front of that camera in a film studio,' recalled Diana.

However, the part was that of a villain's girlfriend, a character older than Diana's fourteen years. But L'Epine Smith encouraged her to say she was 17 instead. When the call came through that morning to say her screen test was that very afternoon at Isleworth Studios, a fuzzy-headed Diana made her way there, still feeling the effects of the alcohol the old admiral had plied her with. She sailed through her scene as if not quite there, the alcohol perhaps cutting through her nerves a bit. The part itself was that of a 'sexy tart', as Diana described it. L'Epine Smith hailed her performance and reassured her that he would reveal her real age at a later date. She won the part and would be paid a handsome sum of £8 a day. The contracts were drawn up with her delighted agent, and fame beckoned at last. There was one problem, however: her name.

Diana's agent had suggested previously that she should change her name. Fluck was rather unusual for a film star and he himself preferred 'Diana Scarlett' after Scarlett O'Hara. Diana was already calling herself Diana Carroll for her modelling work. But Eric L'Epine Smith liked neither and insisted it had to change to something with less 'vulgar' connotations, a comment that enraged Diana's father who was present to sign the contract on her behalf as she was still a minor. It was Diana's mother who suggested Dors, the maiden name of Diana's beloved grandmother.

A bonus was that the alliteration of the double 'D' suited a film star. It was also less risky than seeing the name Fluck in lights at a film premiere and hoping a bulb did not blow. So, Diana Dors was christened and her first film contract was signed.

The Shop at Sly Corner (1946), which is also known by the alternative title, *Code of Scotland Yard*, was directed by George King, known for his earlier Tod Slaughter melodrama adaptations such as the 1936 film, *Sweeney Todd: The Demon Barber of Fleet Street*. Another melodrama, *The Shop at Sly Corner* stars Oskar Homolka, Muriel Pavlow and Derek Farr, with a notable performance by Kenneth Griffith. Homolka plays a wealthy French antiques dealer called Descius Heiss, who is blackmailed by his young shop assistant Archie (Griffith) when he discovers his boss is fencing stolen goods. Diana was cast as Mildred, Archie's girlfriend, who has a taste for the high life. In one particularly pertinent scene, when Homolka's unfortunate antiques dealer visits their flat and spots his own stolen painting, Mildred comments that she doesn't care for it herself as it isn't glamorous enough, adding, 'I love glamour – don't you?' It was a small part, but it got Diana noticed.

Diana's bit of filming took three days, and when she returned home to LAMDA, her classmates treated her with added respect as she was the first of them to appear professionally in a film. More was to follow too, with a call from her agent asking if she could dance the jitterbug. They were casting for *Holiday Camp* at Gainsborough Studios, and needed nifty movers for a dance sequence. Her time spent dancing with the Americans every Saturday night at Bradford Hall in Swindon was finally paying off.

Holiday Camp (1947) is a fun comedy drama directed by the prolific British filmmaker, Ken Annakin, who made nearly fifty films during a successful career spanning decades. Born in Beverley, East Yorkshire, he started making films with the RAF Film Unit during the Second World War, working as a camera operator on notable war propaganda films such as the critically acclaimed *We Serve* (1942), directed by Carol Reed. After a notable documentary career, he later joined Sydney Box at Gainsborough Pictures, having worked with him at Verity Films. *Holiday Camp* was his first feature.

The film stars Flora Robson, Jack Warner, Dennis Price, and Hazel Court, and also features Kathleen Harrison and Jimmy Hanley. Many of the cast would appear in a number of other Gainsborough films. The film is set in a holiday camp, a very popular feature of the British social landscape at the time. The familiar setting resonated with post-war audiences, no doubt adding to its success at the box office. In the film, a working-class London family, the Huggetts, enjoy their first visit to a summer holiday camp. It was the first film to feature the Huggett family, who went on to appear in their own *The Huggetts* film series, in which Diana would later be involved.

Holiday Camp is a delightful kaleidoscope of activity involving the Huggetts and others as they enjoy their holiday time. It captures the feeling and atmosphere of the holiday camp, which was a comfort to the masses in post-war Britain at the time. Like the earlier *Bank Holiday* (Carol Reed, 1938) which was also popular with audiences, the film features an ensemble cast of characters and small stories which run throughout. They include a pregnant young girl and her boyfriend, a jilted sailor, a young woman looking for a husband, a spinster, a pair of card sharps, and a murderer on the run. The film was reportedly based on the experience of writer Godfrey Winn at Butlin's Holiday Camp in Filey, North Yorkshire, and many exteriors were filmed there. Perhaps unusual for the time, the story was developed with creative input from a number of people, and some characters were built around familiar real-life contemporary stories.

A big success at the British box office, *Holiday Camp* gave audiences what they wanted: a little bit of escapism but through a lens of familiarity, with ordinary people doing ordinary things. In Brian MacFarlane's *An Autobiography of British Cinema*, the film's director, Ken Annakin, attributed this in part to the focus on a typical family, 'The Huggetts absolutely caught the spirit and feeling that existed after the war... People did not want more fairy stories; they wanted something in which they could recognise themselves...I think I caught the spirit of the holiday camps and we had a very warm, natural cast.'

Diana did not really have a part as such – she was just one of the crowd – but she loved the experience of being in a film studio again and revelling in the unique atmosphere. Her dance hall scene involved a large crowd of performers, so the place was really buzzing. Her dance partner was the young actor, John Blythe, with whom Diana would appear later in her career for several of her films for the J. Arthur Rank Organisation.

Another film role under her belt, Diana returned triumphantly to LAMDA to sit her gold medal for acting exam. But as well as concentrating on her studies, she also focused her attention on a new boy at the Academy, Geoffrey Loach. At 19, he was older than the now 15-year-old Diana, and yet again she fell in love instantly. He was more worldly-wise than her and their time together felt exhilarating and full of fun. He was ambitious, but ever so slightly wild. He had a wicked sense of humour, which Diana adored, and this in turn would set the tone for future relationships. He encouraged her to push her acting skills at LAMDA to the limit, to try new and challenging roles beyond the restricted range she usually attempted. Loach ruled the roost in their circle of friends from the Academy, his fellow young actors hanging on his every word and action, and Diana herself worshipped him. They double-dated with Diana's roommate and her boyfriend from the Academy. There were trips to the local cinema or walks in Hyde Park, which often ended with frustrated trysts on uncomfortable park benches.

Her encounters with Loach also served as her first real introduction to the mysterious world of sex. Despite her modelling encounters with inappropriate older men, the dancing with American GIs back in Swindon and her outward show of sophistication, at 15, Diana was completely inexperienced and downright frightened by the thought of sex. Her mother had warned her of the dangers of fornication and the chance of having a baby. Oh, the disgrace an illegitimate child born to a teenage mother could bring to the family! Of course, her mother never actually discussed the practicalities and feelings of sex with her, waving away any questions with recourse to it being a horrible experience for a woman, culminating only with the horrors of childbirth and with no talk of pleasure. Her father often reminded her that men thought terribly of girls who made themselves available as 'easy meat', and that every respectable young woman should be a virgin on her wedding night. No wonder Diana was scared.

Yet she desired Loach greatly and confused herself emotionally not knowing the right thing to do. But she heeded her parents' warnings, the worry of an unwanted pregnancy stopping any thoughts of showing her boyfriend how much she really liked him during those passionate park bench interludes. Loach was not happy with her resistance, leaving her feeling unsophisticated and boring compared to other girls. They had done it, so why wouldn't she? Yet she continued to resist, despite his impassioned advances towards her. During the Christmas break, they wrote a number of flamboyant love letters to each other. Her Grandma with the teapots asked if Loach was going to be the one she would marry. The lovestruck Diana truly thought he was, with them becoming the ultimate showbusiness couple and living happily ever after, finally free to enjoy themselves physically as a married couple. The romantic notions of youth enveloped her during the seasonal break.

With the spring term at LAMDA on the horizon, Diana returned to London to act in another film, playing a dance hall hostess in *Dancing with Crime*, a distinctly British film noir directed by John Paddy Carstairs, whose prolific career included film and television work in a variety of genres, but most notably light film comedy. He directed a number of Norman Wisdom films in the 1950s, and other British comedy films of the mid-twentieth century period, including *A Weekend with Lulu* (1961) starring Bob Monkhouse, Leslie Phillips, Shirley Eaton and Irene Handl.

Dancing with Crime (1947) stars a young Richard Attenborough alongside Sheila Sim, Barry K. Barnes and Bill Owen in an early role. Attenborough plays Ted, an ex-army boy back on civvy street, who wants to make a go of things and marry his sweetheart. His mate Dave, played by Owen, falls in with the wrong crowd when he seeks an opportunity to make easy money, but Ted refuses to go along with his plans. Again, Diana plays a small side role with a handful of lines as Annette, a dance hall hostess.

The film was shot at Twickenham Studios during the coldest winter for fifty years. The temperatures were frightful and there was an electricity strike on during filming, so the cast arrived frozen and frustrated, sometimes having their make-up applied by candlelight. Diana endured a 4.30 am start every day, pulling on the hand-me-down winter coat she had inherited from her mother's friend and making her way through the cold to the underground at Earls Court to begin the long journey on public transport to the film studio. Hardly the chauffeur-driven car and special treatment she had imagined a film star would experience. But despite the trials she endured, Diana's fee was fixed at £10 a day to be paid in cash, and after two weeks of filming, she walked away with a £150 fortune.

A few months after she finished filming *Dancing with Crime*, Diana was sent to Gainsborough Studios to do a screen test with producer Sydney Box for a film called *Streets Paved with Water*. Diana was tested for one of the lead roles, alongside Maxwell Reed, Jane Hylton and Andrew Crawford. She was delighted to win the part. When filming began, Diana found she enjoyed every minute, describing her role as a 'very showy one'. However, after a month, the production was suspended. Despite Diana and the rest of the cast being told it had only been postponed due to internal studio politics, it never began again, leaving Diana disappointed.

Back at LAMDA, things with Loach had taken a decidedly colder turn as his ardour was set on another girl now. A heartbroken Diana focused all her attention on her studies and gaining her acting diploma. With three films under her belt already, she was feeling confident about her career. At the end of term, Wilfred Foulis, the head of the Academy, awarded her the London Films Cup, which had been presented to LAMDA by Alexander Korda, the renowned filmmaker. The awards ceremony took place in front of an audience in the Academy's own theatre and leading film star of the time, Greta Gynt, made the presentation of the cup to Diana for 'the girl most likely to succeed in British films.' Their paths would cross again in the future, but at that moment Diana accepted the cup graciously from Greta with a thank you speech prepared by her father. She later admitted that despite the acquisition of medals and awards being the ultimate goal at LAMDA, she discovered that these merits meant very little in the real world of acting: 'It wasn't until I met a casting director a year or so later that I realised to my dismay that one might just as well have acquired a dustbin lid for all the effect it has on the powers-that-be in show business.' However, in that moment on stage collecting her prized merit cup, she was ready to take the next step to stardom.

The Shop at Sly Corner had been released, and Diana took great pleasure in watching herself on the big screen for the first time, which she found to be an amazing experience. It caused quite a stir back home in Swindon too; her name appeared on posters around town and she was asked to make a personal appearance at the film's opening night. Dressed in a beautiful evening gown, Diana was driven to the cinema in Swindon with her dinner-suited father as her escort. Before the screening, she took to the stage to deliver the same speech she had given at LAMDA, her parents looking on proudly from the stalls.

As Diana pondered her next career move, her agent telephoned with news. She did not have to wait long for her next break. It was a screen test for David Lean's *Oliver Twist*. She made her way immediately to Pinewood Studios to test for the role of Charlotte, the maid from the coffin-maker's shop. Diana was thrilled at the prospect of working for Lean. She was prepared by wardrobe and make-up, walking in for her screen test in full Dickensian clothes and with dirt smeared authentically on her face.

Despite her Dickensian attire, she caught the attention of a handsome young showrunner called Kipp, who promptly asked her out. They met the next evening in his hometown of Ruislip. But instead of a genial trip to the cinema or for a meal, Kipp took her to the local woods with only one thing on his mind. Despite his best efforts, he was disappointed and Diana had another lesson in the ways of men.

Returning home one weekend, she was greeted by her excited mother who told her the part in *Oliver Twist* was hers. Not only that, famous film studio executive, J. Arthur Rank, had offered Diana a ten-year contract with a small weekly wage that would increase over time as the contract progressed. Diana could not believe it, her joy at the news shared even by her father who was not normally one to show his emotions. However, he still gave his usual cautionary lecture on the need to work hard. But the contract with Rank, which had an annual option to cancel, was duly signed and a bank account was opened for Diana. No more carrying cash through the streets of London in a suitcase at the end of a week's work like on her previous film assignments. Her father would handle the money, so Diana could concentrate on making films. She was just 15, after all.

Diana had a wonderful experience filming *Oliver Twist* (1948), David Lean's critically acclaimed take on the Charles Dickens classic. Regarded as one of his best films, Lean had previously taken on *Great Expectations* in 1946 with equal success. Lean's *Oliver Twist* is a visual treat of a film, with lavish and detailed settings given as much attention as the sharp script and acting. Old London is portrayed with realism but dusted with artistic flair. It is sooty and dirty but spectacular; given the time in which the film was made, it is testament to Lean's ambition and determination to bring a whole city to the screen that makes it a legendary moment in British film. Much of Dickens' original text is lacking from the film, with whole characters omitted, but this doesn't detract from the success of the production. Often featuring in lists of the greatest films, *Oliver Twist* is much-loved by audiences and often referenced by film writers as a great work. It was also a big success at the box office at the time of its release. This was an important role for the young Diana Dors.

Sir Alec Guinness stars as Fagin and gives a performance that would go down in film history as a tour de force lesson in nuanced theatricality and measured melodrama. But it has caused controversy too, with critics citing the use of heavy prosthetics and suggestions of anti-Semitism in the writing and portrayal of Fagin's character. The character of Oliver is played by John Howard Davies, who gives an understated performance in the role, but one that has informed many subsequent portrayals and parodies of the character. It is perhaps his heartfelt pleas of 'Please sir, I want some more' that audiences recall. The other male lead role of Bill Sikes is played very effectively by Robert Newton, and Kay Walsh stars as Nancy. Diana plays Charlotte, a maid in the coffin-maker's shop. Her role is small but it had a big impact, and she won praise from those in the business for her professional performance. She looked the picture of a Dickensian urchin with her innocent young face but sparky nature, perfect for the spirit of the film. There is also a playful turn by a young actor called Anthony Newley as the Artful Dodger. It would not be the last time Newley and Diana would appear together.

This was a real turning point for Diana to have won such a coveted place in a film as well-made and respected as *Oliver Twist* so early in her career. She had a wonderful time working on the film, describing it as a tremendous experience for someone her age. She recalled later that her costume and make-up were so effective that people did not realise it was her. Once filming ended, Diana prepared to attend the Rank Organisation's school for young actors in Highbury, and another exciting chapter in her acting story was about to begin.

Chapter 3

Joining the Rank 'Charm School'

When Diana Dors walked into the offices of the Rank Organisation in 1947 at the age of 15, she was unaware of just how important a step it would be in her career.

J. Arthur Rank was an unusual movie mogul to say the least. A devout, teetotal Methodist and Sunday school teacher, he made a fortune in the flour industry before venturing into film with the intention of making religious pictures and spreading the word of God. He was a conservative man in deeds and his politics, and very rarely went to the cinema. He joined the Guilds of Light which distributed film projectors for religious teachings, and rose within its ranks to the point where he exerted enough control to rename it the Religious Film Society and start on a path of modest film production. Rank effectively assumed control of the General Film Distributors organisation, before founding Pinewood Studios and buying up Denham Studios from its creditors. Elstree followed. He gained control of Gaumont, and then a string of Art Deco Odeon cinemas after the death of founder Oscar Deutsch in 1941, to secure an outlet for his own religious film output. The Second World War saw audiences flocking to the cinema to escape the realities of wartime Britain and his business empire grew.

The late 1940s was a golden age in British film production and Rank was involved in the majority of it, presumably assuaging his initial religious motivations for entering the industry. As well as maintaining his empire, he also gave financial support to the likes of Ealing Studios during their triumphant run of film classics such as the lauded Ealing Comedy series and the influential work of Powell and Pressburger. There were many more productions which benefited from his deep pockets too. It was not all plain sailing as he made some enemies in the process, and naivety on his part meant many directors took artistic licence and advantage, which did not help matters financially for the organisation. By the late 1940s, focus shifted to smaller, less expensive films with a range of performers on contract to the company. And by the early 1950s, Rank himself stepped away from overseeing film production matters, placing the controversial but financially astute figure of John Davis at the helm. Davis was an accountant by trade who, according to one writer was, 'An intolerant dictator, who was ill-suited to the business of film production,' and was ruthless in his bid to eliminate rivals to the Rank empire.

Diana signed a contract with the Rank Organisation's 'Charm School' for young actors, a scheme to produce stars of the future. Officially known as The Company of Youth, but soon nicknamed a charm school, it was a deliberate attempt by J. Arthur Rank to manufacture glamorous film stars in a similar way to the Hollywood studio system, albeit based in a draughty church hall in Highbury. He was also reportedly encouraged by the success of Gainsborough Pictures in developing British stars such as Stewart Granger, James Mason and Phyllis Calvert.

Film producer Sydney Box had originally set up a Company of Youth at Riverside Studios in late 1945. He put a small group of young actors under contract and then placed them in minor film roles while they were learning their acting craft. When he was recruited by Rank in 1946, Box transferred his original company to Gainsborough. The Rank Charm School operated from a church hall next to the company's 'B picture' studio in Highbury. Students were given a small weekly allowance. In his book *Searching for Stars*, film journalist Geoffrey MacNab described the school as 'a sort of cross between Lee Strasberg's Actors Studio and a London finishing school for young ladies'.

Alongside a pool of talented young hopefuls all dreaming of stardom, including Christopher Lee, Petula Clark, Joan Collins and Claire Bloom, Diana was to be groomed for success. The school's main acting teacher was Molly Terraine. As well as artistic techniques such as reading a play, script study, diction, movement and mime, there were 'behavioural lessons' in etiquette and deportment, intended to add a touch of grace and poise to the rough-around-the-edges but fame-hungry youngsters who walked through the doors. The school was a machine for spotting and shaping talent, then churning them out into the studio system as quickly and often as possible.

Although excited at the prospect of attending, Diana was a little underwhelmed by its less-than-glamorous location. She also felt that attending was a waste of time for someone like herself, who had appeared in films and won awards for her acting at LAMDA. She had a rather rude awakening when she realised that her medals did not matter to anyone out in the real world. But each and every day in the long, hot summer of 1947, she climbed aboard the number 19 bus to Highbury with the other Rank starlets and journeyed to the dreary church hall to be 'paid to learn.'

Diana proved to be very popular at Rank. She was not afraid to show her willingness to succeed, including agreeing to be photographed attending film premieres and parties, and taking part in photo shoots. As a result, she received a lot of attention and publicity, and was nicknamed 'The Body' in a 1947 Australian newspaper article. In 1949, another journalist referred to her as 'Diana Dors, five-foot-five of charm and sparkle with long soft fair hair and blue eyes…This provocative young thing.'

She would later describe her experience at the Charm School as a frustrating one. After the period she spent learning her craft at LAMDA, 'I frankly felt that it was all rather a waste of time.' She could see the value for other members of the company, 'Some of whom had been found in beauty contests and who had been given film contracts without even being able to read properly.' She was certainly a spirited member of the group, often found getting up on tables and singing. She was criticised for her behaviour outside of class by her teachers, including walking down the local streets in skimpy clothing and spitting out cherry stones into the gutter. These were both a big no-no as far as the management were concerned.

Now Diana had a prized studio contract, she went on to appear in many of the Rank Organisation's films. She had a small role in melodrama *The Calendar* (1948), an adaptation of an Edgar Wallace novel, directed by Arthur Crabtree and starring Greta Gynt and John McCallum. Diana plays a maid who mainly serves tea to Gynt, who had presented Diana with her acting cup just a few months previously at LAMDA. She also had a short, scene-stealing appearance in *It's Not Cricket* (1949) as a rather flirty candidate for a secretarial job at a struggling detective agency, running rings around the two stars, Basil Radford and Naunton Wayne.

This film appearance was followed hot on the heels by a part in intense noir drama *Good-Time Girl* (1948) as troubled teen Lyla Lawrence. Directed by David MacDonald, the film is based on Arthur La Bern's novel *Night Darkens the Street* and starred Jean Kent, Dennis Price and Herbert Lom. Kent plays Gwen Rawlings, a teenage girl who falls in with the wrong crowd. Diana's character, Lyla, risks a similar fate. It is notable that her character, although relatively minor, bookends the film as she is seen being warned about a life of trouble at the start by the chair of the juvenile court (played by Flora Robson), and heeding that warning in the closing scene.

Badged as a 'notable box office attraction', the film was initially banned by the British film censors for its questionable language. It was the first of Diana's films to court controversy, perhaps setting the tone of things to come. She also had a small role as the wonderfully named 'Dreary Girl' in *My Sister and I* (1948).

A bigger part was to follow in thriller *Penny and the Pownall Case* (1948), directed by Harry 'Slim' Hand and starring Ralph Michael, Peggy Evans and a young Christopher Lee. As a sign of her progress, Diana had fourth billing, an amazing achievement for the young star. A somewhat routine pot-boiler detective yarn, the story focuses on escaped German Second World War prisoners in early post-war Britain and a glamour model, played by Evans, who helps Scotland Yard to capture the criminal gang trying to smuggle them out of Europe. Diana, who still had darker hair at the time, plays a dowdy young secretary called Molly James. Her image is purposely contrasted with the stereotypical sexy, blonde female lead portrayed by Evans, which would soon become a familiar type of role for Diana herself.

The film was an unusual prospect for Rank. At just 45 minutes long it is barely feature-length, and was made by their subsidiary, Highbury Productions, as a short 'curtain-raiser' for other Rank features. Lee later described it as a 'Z feature', a bit of an un-professional free-for-all, and commented that he felt embarrassed by it and his performance. It also turned out to be Hand's only outing as a director – he usually worked as a production manager at Ealing Studios. But the film is notable for the involvement of composer Elisabeth Lutyens, making her the first female British composer to score a feature film.

However, it was not an experience Diana enjoyed, especially when the director apparently rebuked her for questioning him when he insisted her secretary character would take down shorthand without ever looking at her notepad. She also was not keen on the 6 am starts on set, nor the fact she was asked to cut her beloved long, thick hair. Her protestations on this point were met with derision back at the Charm School. Molly Terraine, the head acting coach, lambasted her, 'What kind of an actress do you call yourself? Do you think Laurence Olivier enjoys walking around Denham with dyed blonde hair while he's playing Hamlet?'

During this time, while at Denham Studios for an unsuccessful screen test for an adaptation of Mary Webb's 1924 novel *Precious Bane*, Diana met and fell for another man. She was sat having her make-up removed when in walked a tall, dark-haired and handsome man with a booming masculine voice, demanding to see her. In her autobiography, she recounts his introductory words, 'So *you* are Diana Dors. Everyone's talking about you, so I thought I'd come and have a look for myself…Not bad!' In a whirlwind of charming banter, she managed to discover that he too had been there for a screen test for a leading role in the film and that he too was under contract at Rank. Guy Rolfe was not a Charm School starlet like her; he was a confident and experienced older man, and already a star in his own right. He promptly offered the teenaged Diana a lift back to London in his car.

As he pulled up outside the YWCA, Diana felt quite ashamed and embarrassed, and self-conscious about her young age. Rolfe teased her about her curfew, and about her living in an 'institution' but asked her out to dinner the next evening. His ego did not even question whether she might be free to go on a date with him. But Diana was hooked already, dreamily telling her friend when she arrived back in her room that she had met the most wonderful man. Not once did the young Diana think that Guy Rolfe, a man in his thirties, might be attached or even married.

Sure enough, the next evening they dined at a Soho restaurant, which made quite a change from her previous park bench dates. Afterwards, he took her back to his flat nearby. Diana recalls that he made no move on her that evening, nor on subsequent evenings they spent together. He found her virginity fascinating rather than something to challenge. With the benefit of hindsight, however, an older Diana recalled the inappropriateness of their relationship. Rolfe was 37, she at that time was 15. He started to treat her to what amounted to emotional and psychological bullying, commenting on the way she looked, spoke and behaved, and giving her a complex about herself. Nothing she did or said passed without sarcastic comment. He was, of course, married. His wife was also an actress and at that time appearing in a play near to the flat. No wonder Diana was swept home promptly each evening – he needed to be back at the stage door to collect his wife.

As time went on, their regular-as-clockwork weekday dates sometimes did not happen, leaving a heartbroken and confused Diana waiting by the phone in her YWCA for his call that often did not come. Her bus from the Charm School passed by his flat, and she would find herself staring up at it, trying to work out if the faint shadows at the window could be him and his wife, or perhaps another girl. Guy had a powerful and manipulative hold over her. On her sixteenth birthday she waited by the phone for him to call, dressed up and excited about what he might have planned for her. But there was no call. He did call the next day and they went out to dinner, followed by time spent in his flat. As she left, he gave her money: 'That's for your birthday. I know how you must have felt when I did not call. It's a terrible thing for a child to have its birthday forgotten.'

Perhaps too young to understand the complexity of just how unsuitable their relationship was, she was well aware of his callousness and that his treatment made her feel worthless. Their relationship fizzled out and Diana struggled to get over the emotional upheaval Rolfe had caused in her life. She reflected much later that, 'I was totally in awe of him and for six months whilst he amused himself with my emotions, I went through all the traumas a girl can expect to feel when associating with a man who already has a wife.' She recalls meeting him again years later when she was at the peak of her film career. Over lunch she challenged him to think about the fact he had known her since she was 15, and she was now approaching 30. But Rolfe laughed the inquiry off, saying it just made him feel old. Diana was in no doubt that his antics had not changed that much in the intervening years.

The moral ambiguity and behavioural pressures around sex would continue to dominate Diana's early film career. The balance between opportunity and impropriety was hard to navigate. Diana was attractive and was noticed. But she was young and vulnerable to the behaviours of those more senior or influential than her. In her autobiography, she recalls a weekly cocktail party thrown for all the Rank Charm School starlets by David Henley, who was nominally responsible for the running of the place (although most in the industry knew it was actually Rank's Head of Contract Artists, Olive Dodds, who did the real work). This event provided the opportunity for the young actors to mingle with film directors, studio executives and producers in the hope of being spotted.

Diana suggests there was always an unwritten rule about 'services rendered'. She indicates that she herself was saved from this assumption by Sydney Box, the producer at Gainsborough Studios who had given Diana her first film role. He had apparently given word to the men who attended these events that as she was under 16, she was 'off limits'. However, a while later, she recalls being summoned to see a top film producer in his office one evening to discuss an opportunity. Obviously alone, Diana was asked to undress so he could assess how much 'puppy fat' she still had, given that she was still very young. She was saved only by the producer's secretary arriving and he quickly dismissed Diana from his office, telling her to keep working hard at the Charm School. When she recounted the incident to her disappointed parents, not telling of the request to undress, of course, just the comments about her weight, her father responded, 'A man in that position wouldn't bother to speak with you for such a trivial reason. It's quite obvious that you're not concentrating on your work properly.' He went on to warn her that she might be dropped if she was not careful. The pressure bore down heavily on Diana's young shoulders, her behaviour continually either under scrutiny or challenged by those with authority over her. Like many young women of her generation, she evidently could not win.

However, her original mentor Sydney Box would intervene again to right her career path, providing her with her biggest screen role yet. It was a supporting role in *Here Come the Huggetts (1948)*, the first part of a popular comedy film series made by Gainsborough and directed by Ken Annakin, about a working-class English family. The film stars Jack Warner and Kathleen Harrison as factory worker Joe Huggett and his wife Ethel, with their spirited young daughters played by Petula Clark, Jane Hylton and Susan Shaw. The film was inspired by the characters in the earlier *Holiday Camp* from 1947, in which Diana did the jitterbug early in her career. Warner plays the quintessential cinema father figure in Joe, and the Huggetts became a symbol for the everyday family.

The Huggetts film series was a big box office success for Gainsborough, though perhaps not with the critics. After the warm reception given to the working-class Huggett family in *Holiday Camp*, the later spin-off films changed the configuration slightly, keeping the popular Joe and Ethel, but replacing the original son and daughter (played by Peter Hammond and Hazel Court) with three teenage daughters instead: Jane (Hylton), Susan (Shaw) and Pet (Clark). Confusingly, Peter Hammond was recast in the later films as Jane's boyfriend. Additional repeat characters were added, including Grandma Huggett (Amy Veness) and the character played by Diana, a flighty young cousin of Ethel's, also called Diana.

The first Huggetts film was quickly followed by two further outings for the family, *Vote for Huggett*, in which Joe stands for local election, and *The Huggetts Abroad*, which sees the family emigrate to South Africa and inadvertently become involved in smuggled diamonds. Both films were released in 1949. All the films in the series were directed by Annakin, who had also directed the original *Holiday Camp*, and produced by Betty E. Box, the sister of Sydney Box. Like the successful *Holiday Camp*, the films had a number of writers working in collaboration, including then husband and wife team, Sydney and Muriel Box. Muriel Box went on to forge a writing and directing career in the 1950s and 1960s, producing notable works that often depicted the female experience, despite the prejudices and barriers experienced by female filmmakers at the time.

The Huggetts had quite a large cultural impact. One film reviewer from the time noted that the film series, 'Relies for its appeal on its homely humour and fine characterisations' from its main players, as well as a strong supporting cast. In addition to the films, a BBC radio series called *Meet the Huggetts* ran from 1953 to 1962. This radio version saw both Warner and Harrison reprising the roles of Joe and Ethel, but again their family consisted of different members, now with one daughter, Jane (played by Marion Collins) and a son called Bobby (George Howell), rather than the three sisters of the film series, or the original son and daughter of *Holiday Camp*. Apparently, there was another film version planned, *Christmas with the Huggetts*, but this was never made.

In *Here Come the Huggetts*, Diana was cast as Ethel's younger cousin Diana, who arrives for a decidedly unwelcome family visit. She ends up wreaking havoc at home and in Joe's factory when he is persuaded to bag her a job there. The film also stars Anthony Newley as one of the daughters' boyfriends. Newley was now also under contract with Rank.

This was a delightful role for Diana. She was partnered again with John Blythe, with whom she had danced in *Holiday Camp*, and they made quite an amusing duo. Her character was also quite opinionated, with an attitude considered quite modern for the time. The film showcased her wonderful comic acting too, and she would go on to appear in the follow-up film in the series, *Vote for Huggett* (1949), again partnered with Blythe. Her portrayal of the 'troublesome niece' Diana would set the tone for a number of her subsequent film appearances as the rather disruptive and cheeky presence in ensemble casts. But her role in both films was apparently appreciated by audiences, and critics acknowledged her impact as the 'vampish' niece giving 'showy comic support', with *The Monthly Film Bulletin* even commenting on her fine characterisation.

Diana was delighted with her time on *Here Come the Huggetts*. She felt her part gave her a lot to do, and it felt like a turning point. Diana took her mother Mary along to the press screening, excited to be sharing such an important moment in her burgeoning career. They laughed along together, both pleased with Diana's performance in what felt to them to be an enjoyable film. Although Diana and Mary loved it, the critics did not. Instead of rushing over to congratulate her on a wonderful performance, they were decidedly stony-faced. After that embarrassing disappointment, Diana made the decision there and then never to attend another press screening for one of her films, and apparently stuck to it for the rest of her career.

With the release of David Lean's much-lauded adaptation of *Oliver Twist* that year, 1948 was to be the making of Diana as performer. With *Oliver Twist*, she was able to shed her usual glossy persona; previous roles had perhaps not given the opportunity for her acting ability to shine through. She was 'deglamorised' in the role of Charlotte, a downtrodden maid-of-all-work, and it allowed her to show her nuanced and intelligent characterisation. It was a triumph, so much so that Rank himself announced that same year that she was to be one of the half a dozen young actors chosen from his self-styled academy that he wanted to build up into a star. Those tentative first steps into the limelight that she took with her first films for the Rank Organisation would prove to be the start of something exciting, and it was clear Diana had a bright future ahead of her.

Indeed, she was on the verge of another great opportunity. She had an appointment with director Ralph Smart at Gainsborough Studios. Smart, who Diana later described as, 'A plump, jolly man who seemed more like a games teacher than a director,' wanted to speak to her regarding a film he was making about cycling clubs called *A Boy, a Girl and a Bike* (1949). The film was to be shot mostly on location in the beautiful Yorkshire Dales, and Diana was being considered for the 'bad girl' role of Ada Foster. But this was a part that would receive top support billing, just beneath the stars of the film, John McCallum, Patrick Holt and young rising star Honor Blackman, who had recently signed with Rank. Diana was delighted to be given the role.

The romantic light comedy about the various escapades of a Yorkshire cycling club, the fictional Wakeford Wheelers, features several boys, girls and bicycles, and a number of convoluted subplots. Blackman plays Sue, who is engaged to fellow cyclist Sam (Patrick Holt), but as they have not found anywhere to live yet, their engagement is a bit on the informal side. The rather posher and slightly arrogant David, played by John McCallum, who is the son of a local, arrives on the scene. Smitten with Sue, he joins the club and pursues her with all his energies, much to the dismay of local boy Sam.

Unusual for the time in its use of location shooting, the film depicts leisure pursuits popular with regular working-class cinema audiences: cycling and dancing. It was a wonderful prospect for Diana, and an opportunity to enjoy a location shoot in Yorkshire, somewhere she had never been before.

A car was hired by the studio to take her to King's Cross Station to catch the train north. She was travelling up with Anthony Newley, and they were accompanied by the film's producer, Bunny Keene, who was responsible for escorting the young actors to Yorkshire. As the two youngest contract actors on the Rank books, they were precious cargo. Diana and Newley got on well. Although they were both 16, she thought him too young for her romantically, but had been very impressed by his acting skills as the Artful Dodger in *Oliver Twist*.

Diana fell in love with Yorkshire instantly. The magnificence of the beautiful scenery quite overwhelmed her as they made their way to the Fell Hotel near Grassington to join the rest of the cast and crew. The experience of filming was still a delightful novelty for Diana, and she loved every minute of her time working on location. Filming started early each day to catch the morning sun, but she did not mind. She also accepted the long hours. The weariness at the end of each day was not a problem, because she was enchanted by the whole experience and that was part of it. She also enjoyed the camaraderie on set and the feeling of togetherness, away from home, which was unique and new to her. Some of the lead actors and main production crew had their wives and husbands staying with them, while some of the younger cast and crew enjoyed the flirting and hooking up which came with the experience of being away from home. As Diana acknowledged, marital status was not always a consideration. Romance blossomed and relationships formed. What happened on location stayed on location.

Diana formed an unlikely friendship with a more experienced male actor during filming, although she didn't specify who it was. Often, she would seek his advice, and not just regarding acting. She was still feeling confused and conflicted about relationships and sex, and asked him what men thought of girls who slept with them before marriage. Diana recalled that he patiently listened, showed understanding and gave sensible and measured advice, something she had been lacking up until that time. She found it helpful, understanding that she should think what it was that she wanted and needed, both emotionally and physically.

Romance did inevitably blossom on set for Diana as she fell for a Norwegian member of the camera crew named Gil. He was tall, blonde and handsome, and not afraid to show his sun-tanned physique on the hot days during filming. Gil also happened to be the brother of Greta Gynt. He was a serious young man and Diana later referred to him as a 'sun-bronzed iceberg'. But what he lacked in the usual cheeky humour that she normally went for, he made up with raw sex appeal and he was popular with many of the younger women on set. But as they spent time together, things moved on for Diana and Gil. After long days of filming, they would stroll hand in hand on those balmy summer evenings, their attraction for each other evident. During a dance laid on by the film company, Diana seethed with jealousy when she saw Gil dancing with another girl. She ran to her room, upset and frustrated, only for Gil to knock on her door. The moment had come for Diana to give herself completely to someone she desired; it was what she wanted and it felt right. However, she did wonder afterwards what all the fuss was about!

Their romance continued throughout filming. Diana felt she was living in some sort of wonderland up in Yorkshire and she never wanted the experience to end. She had no wish to return to smoky old London as her heart was won by the fresh air and lush beauty of Yorkshire. She created in her mind a romantic idyll, imagining setting up home with Gil there, a never-ending sweet summer. Lying together by the edge of streams and on riverbanks, silent but for the sounds of nature around them, and gazing at vistas of purple gorse-covered hills in the distance. A far cry from the reality of life in the YWCA back home.

Sadly, the day came when location shooting completed and the crew began to pack up, ready to return to London and begin interior scenes in the studios. The fantasy was over. Diana had to face the reality of her return to London and her old routines of early morning alarm calls and traipsing through dreary London streets. But Diana hatched a plan to find a flat of her own.

The thought of the freedom having her own space could bring fizzed in Diana's head. She would be free of the restrictions of the YWCA: no more sharing rooms with other girls and she could wave goodbye to the early morning alarm call. After the independence she enjoyed during the location shoot in Yorkshire, she just could not go back to the conditions she had endured. After a feverish search, she found a furnished flat just off the King's Road in Chelsea for five guineas a week. It was small but perfectly formed, with a living room, bedroom, bathroom and kitchen. It might not be a Hollywood mansion, but to Diana it was perfect. When she opened the door to that flat, she was walking into a whole new chapter of her life.

Not unexpectedly, her parents were horrified. Even her mother strongly objected to her living on her own, rather than in the secure hostel they had arranged for her. But Diana was now 16 and financially independent. She did not dwell on her other reasons for craving her own space, of course. Again, Yorkshire had opened her eyes to a world of possibilities in terms of her own emotional affairs too. At the back of her mind, she was thinking this would be a love nest for her and Gil, and as soon as she moved in, she made sure to invite him back after a dinner date. Things with Gil felt different in London though. He seemed distant. She was sure he was not married, but it felt that inevitably their summer romance had cooled. Diana felt hugely disappointed to finally have her freedom and a love nest to be proud of, yet she had nobody to share it with. The next day, she arrived on set to film some of the remaining interior shots for *A Boy, a Girl and a Bike* distinctly under a cloud. What she was not banking on was Anthony Newley declaring his love for her.

She had very much enjoyed Newley's company on location. But with her head full of her infatuation with Gil, she had not really acknowledged how handsome he was. He was talented and full of personality too, just Diana's type. She fell for him in an instant. They were both 16, financially independent of their parents and under contract to a film studio. Their sense of responsibility inevitably flew out of the window. Diana later reflected that during that period of her life she was always, 'In love again, out of love again, displaying the ebullience of youth.' There were endless parties at Diana's Chelsea flat. On one occasion, Diana recalled Newley took twenty-seven takes to finish a scene the morning after a particularly heavy party session.

Later on, Diana acknowledged that their studio contracts often meant that they were under-utilised as actors, and left to their own devices.

Too much free time, too much spare cash and a lack of close supervision inevitably led to typical teenage behaviour outside of filming. This was a situation that was often commented on by the more experienced actors they worked with at the time. Diana's flat became party central for the pair and their friends. Their relationship was tempestuous and Diana found Newley to be temperamental and unpredictable. They would often row, make up, then find themselves back to square one again. The path of young love did not run smoothly.

Despite her turbulent personal life, Diana was still making progress with her film career and she was about to win her first starring role. The director David MacDonald wanted to make what he considered to be the first British 'Western', *Diamond City* (1949). Set in the diamond fields of nineteenth-century South Africa and based on actual events, the film tells the story of a British entrepreneur who, when a diamond field is discovered in South Africa, attempts to exploit it while maintaining law and order in town in near-anarchy and bringing about a peaceful settlement with the local Boer leaders.

There are not many examples of Westerns in British cinema, and *Diamond City* was a brave attempt to fill that gap. Whether it really counts as a Western, being set in South Africa, is still up for debate. But it tried to recreate the Western sentiment and atmosphere, albeit with a rather British feel. The proven Western ingredients are all present, and if they were mining for gold instead of diamonds, you could imagine it was set on the unforgiving American plains rather than the Transvaal terrain. There is a historical bent to the film, with its attempt to depict how the British and the Boers came to often uneasy territorial deals. Based on a true story about British artist and miner Stafford Parker, who lived in South Africa's diamond fields in the 1870s, the film was originally set to be made in 1945 with Stewart Granger in the lead role, but that version never came to fruition.

One of the last films to be made before Gainsborough Pictures closed its doors, this second attempt to tell the story of Parker was to star David Farrar, fresh from his success in *Black Narcissus*, Honor Blackman and Jean Kent. Keeping to their usual stereotypes, Blackman was to be cast as a prim and innocent Salvation Army officer, and Kent was to be the sexy bad girl. However, Diana recalled that Kent, who was ten years her senior, decided she did not want to portray yet another sleazy woman so Diana was screen-tested instead.

The role Diana plays is that of Dora Bracken, a hard-bitten saloon hostess who supervises the brawling miners who have rushed to the area to find diamonds. She also provides the initial love interest for Parker, whose head is eventually turned by her love rival, the angelic Mary Hart, played by Blackman. It is a wide-ranging part that requires Diana to sing, dance, play the piano, brawl and banter with the predominantly male bar crowd. The part could so easily have descended into cheap bawdiness, but Diana plays the role with class, providing the character with enough edge to give the men, and her love rival Hart, what for, but still revealing her soft side. Displaying a world-weary maturity beyond her years, her withering looks could curdle milk. In themes that would be echoed throughout her own love life, she also manages to display the vulnerability of a woman destined to fall for the wrong man and not be treated with respect, 'a good sort, but not good enough'. Diana pulled the performance off with aplomb, despite revealing later on that, 'At seventeen, I was trying to play a hard-bitten belle of about thirty. I looked like a little girl dressed up in her mother's clothes.' She gives a convincing and hearty performance, making the most of what was her first real chance to show what she could do with a lead role.

The wrong side of the town is represented by the menacing hard-nut businessman Muller (Niall MacGinnis), whose constant arguments with Farrar's do-gooding Parker supply much of the dramatic tension and melodramatic punch-ups. It is the usual case of good versus evil that runs through every Western, and makes them so familiar and popular with cinema audiences. A bit of brawling, drinking and revelry never harmed anyone either.

Farrar cuts an impressive figure as Parker, a mix of virile and manly grandstanding laced with brooding sensuality. Diana found she had chemistry with Farrar, so much so that apparently the rather brusque director MacDonald called her young morals into question.

Also known for his lavish Gainsborough costume melodramas such as *The Bad Lord Byron* (1949) and *Christopher Columbus* (1949), MacDonald apparently had a bit of a reputation for being rather fierce and unpredictable. But Diana was not intimidated by him, having already worked with him briefly on *Good-Time Girl* (1948) and seemingly enjoyed the experience overall. Filmed on location in the Kimberley region of South Africa with studio work at Denham Studios in London, MacDonald reportedly had the planned twenty-five-day location shoot in South Africa over and done with by day twelve. Diana was unfortunately only required for the shoot at Denham.

Diamond City was a fantastic opportunity and Diana knew she should not waste it. Having reached the grand age of 17, she needed to focus on her work and cut back on the parties. At Christmas 1948, Diana spent time with her extended family in Wales, but all she could think about was getting back to her life in London and starting work on *Diamond City*. She knew she also had to take dance lessons to learn the cancan. Diana just wished for Christmas to be over. By New Year, she was back in Chelsea and its familiar faces and places. New Year's Eve was spent in a Chelsea pub, The Cross Keys, with her friends. It was there that she encountered someone who would become a significant figure in her life.

She spotted Michael Caborn-Waterfield across the crowded bar and was instantly attracted to his good looks. His eyes were piercingly beautiful and struck her straight away. She walked across the room to get to know him and found he was gloriously arrogant. She told him about her role in *Diamond City*, and he countered with a comment about going to Hollywood to star in *The Secret Garden*. Diana felt deflated. He then turned his back on her to talk to his friends again, leaving her furious. She was not going to put up with such treatment from a man! Later that evening, they were at the same party and he was the worse for drink. As Diana recalls, 'We ignored each other studiedly, yet I remained fascinated and still wondered who he was.'

She spotted him again a number of times over the next few weeks and months, often racing up and down the King's Road in various cars. Inevitably, their paths crossed again in the Cross Keys, but this time he was charm personified. He held a real fascination for Diana. Yet again she was swayed by his good looks, but he was intelligent and had a fascinating history. He was titled, his father having been a Count and a leading

Air Commander during the war. He and his brother John were born in Bermuda, their parents being great socialites. When they divorced, the brothers had returned to England with their mother to attend public school. By the age of just 19, Caborn-Waterfield had led a colourful life. He was attempting to be an actor, and oozed confidence and swagger. He was a man about town, and seemingly knew everyone there was to know. He apparently sailed along on the crest of a wave of good fortune.

At 17, this was not Diana's first taste of what she thought was love, and she thought she knew what it was all about. She finished things with Newley, determined that Caborn-Waterfield was the one for her. But she would soon learn the subtle differences between love and infatuation. 'To be in love with someone and to love unselfishly with all one's heart and soul are two different things,' she later said.

Their early days together were a whirlwind of non-stop parties and nightclubs, all-consuming fun and excitement. Even when she started work on *Diamond City*, she did not let it interfere with her active social life, despite her good intentions when she won the part. Diana, Michael, his friend Patrick, and Oona, Diana's stand-in on the film set, would go straight out on the town after each day's filming had concluded. Diana would only be in bed for a couple of hours a night before being picked up to go on set at 6.30 am. But she was oblivious to it, happy that she was in love and she was making films. The obvious signs of overdoing it, however, were inevitably starting to show on her face as she staggered into the make-up chair. The hectic social life and heavy days of filming took their toll and Diana collapsed on set. The studio sent her back to Swindon by car, wrapped in a blanket and obviously exhausted. Her parents had been rather worried about her anyway because she had barely been home at weekends and at that moment, their fears seemed entirely justified.

Diana's mother Mary nursed her for two weeks. Caborn-Waterfield, who Diana had not really mentioned to her parents, rang practically every day. Diana recalled that he even told her incredulous mother, 'You've had her for seventeen years. I want her now.'

Feeling rejuvenated after her imposed period of rest, Diana returned to London, only to discover that the lease on her flat was to be terminated. Chelsea's party central was to be closed down, hardly surprising given the overindulgent behaviour of Diana and her Chelsea Set friends. She quickly had to take what she referred to as a 'depressing flatlet' in Jermyn Street. Apparently, you could only see sky if you sat awkwardly with your head out of the window, and it was so dark inside that the lights were left on permanently. It was hardly paradise and it cost even more than the King's Road flat. But the farewell party at the old flat was a cracker.

Despite Caborn-Waterfield deciding to move to Dorset with his friend Patrick and Patrick's now-girlfriend Oona, Diana insisted to her furious mother that she and Michael were not only in love but that they were engaged. He had indeed given her a dress ring in lieu of a real one. Her father was more than furious. He even sent her a letter, stating exactly what he thought of her boyfriend. Diana recalled in her autobiography that it ended, 'It is dreadful for your mother and me to have to sit back and watch what is happening to you…I can only liken it to seeing a child playing on the edge of a cliff, and we are powerless to stop you from falling over.'

By the summer of 1949, Diana had finished work on *Diamond City* and was appearing in *The Cat and the Canary* at the Connaught Theatre in Worthing. At the time, the Rank Organisation had a policy to send its contracted artists to theatres if they were not filming, to appear as part of the repertoire company as a way of keeping their skills topped up. This play was closely followed by a stint in *The Good Young Man* in Hayes.

The Rank Charm School had often been viewed as a bit of a joke, by those in the industry and its own students. It did not help that when they were at a loose end workwise, they were sent off to drum up publicity through photo calls and local appearances. Any pretty face would do. Much of its activity in terms of training seemed to focus on the inconsequential, like how to walk properly, how to smile appropriately and the best way to enter a room. The school often failed to teach its students how to handle the trappings of the fame they courted, which led to some notable falls from grace. Its reputation for not shielding its young female stars from unwanted and unsuitable attention from men in suits and directors did it no favours either. It was a known secret that the young women of its school were viewed as up for grabs. One newspaper article dismissed it as simply a vehicle for 'Grooming beautiful girls into great stars.' Sydney

Box's reported intervention on the then 15-year-old Diana's behalf was perhaps an exception that proved the rule.

Diana herself later admitted that she loathed the Charm School and her time there. She witnessed the effects of the expectations placed on the girls, who she referred to as the 'baby-faced girls with the bodies of mature women', to entertain the producers at parties. Although she commented that she had been largely shielded from it herself, she did not enjoy the long round of personal appearances they had to make either, standing there accepting bouquets in borrowed gowns worn by other young actresses. Most importantly for Diana, she felt she had not been afforded the opportunities she craved to make a big success of her acting career.

Many film producers were increasingly reluctant to work with the young Charm School actors, and in 1951, the Rank Charm School closed its doors. However, the venture uncovered a lot of acting talent, giving work opportunities to many young performers who went on to build successful artistic careers. Some appeared fleetingly in its vicinity, passing through on the way to bigger things. It was certainly an experiment that had an impact.

Diana was joined in Worthing by her mother, and they had quite a jolly time staying by the sea, lodging with a local family. There were disagreements about her engagement to Caborn-Waterfield, of course, and Diana was delighted when she returned to London to discover that his business venture in Dorset – a funfair – had failed and they were all on their way back. He moved in with her in Jermyn Street, having lost all of his money. They lived off her contract money and their love for each other, and their life was frugal but full of fun. Caborn-Waterfield introduced Diana to his mother, but to her disappointment, Diana's father still refused to meet him.

They moved to a better flat in Earls Court, but she was not working and there were no new films on the horizon. *Diamond City* was set to be released, so she was hopeful that directors and producers would see it and realise her star potential. To keep her busy, rather than pay her to do nothing, Rank wanted to send her on a tour of south coast town theatres with the play *Lisette*. There were hopes that after its short tour it might have a run in the West End. Rehearsals commenced in a small room in

Soho, prior to opening in Brighton. But a horrified Diana discovered she was pregnant. Despite her insistence that she needed to quit the play, the producer apparently held her to her contract, insisting she go on. She was horribly sick, both with the pregnancy and the worry about what she would do. There was no way she and Caborn-Waterfield could support a child.

She continued with the short tour, appearing on stage to lukewarm reviews. She returned to London on her eighteenth birthday, relieved that the tour was over and with no sign of a West End run on the cards, she set about dealing with her personal situation. Her parents were oblivious to it, of course. Her friend Oona knew a woman who could help her, but it would cost £10, which was the equivalent of more than £300, a small fortune in 1949 and more than the young couple had left each week to live on. Caborn-Waterfield called his stepmother to ask if she could send money to cover the cost of the abortion. Like many young women of the time, Diana endured the illegal procedure, delivered on the kitchen table of a woman in Battersea.

This was a very dangerous step for Diana to take. Not only was abortion illegal in the United Kingdom in 1949 and punishable by a prison sentence for both the woman and the abortionist, it was also incredibly dangerous. For women with money and status, an abortion would involve a clandestine visit to a willing, trained doctor, who would perform the procedure. But for poor women like Diana, it was a very different story. Contraception in those days was largely inadequate for married and single women. For unmarried women, a baby would also mean social and economic catastrophe.

Many women would try to deal with ending their pregnancies themselves at home, with various methods, such as purging, which were incredibly dangerous and largely unsuccessful. So, women were driven to backstreet abortionists who were usually medically untrained. The procedure would take place in someone's home without anaesthetic, using old or inadequate surgical instruments that had not been sterilised. Like the one Diana endured, such abortions were agonising. Fatalities were a huge risk, and there was also the risk of infection and secondary complications. In 1967 the Abortion Act was passed, legalising abortions on certain grounds in the United Kingdom, but not Northern Ireland at that stage; the legislation came into effect in April 1968. For Diana, the procedure led to hours of physical agony, and months of mental and emotional anguish. She had just turned 18.

As she recovered from her ordeal, Diana tried to focus again on her career prospects and look to the future. By Christmas 1949, *Diamond City* had been released. Diana attended the premiere but avoided the press show. The reviews were not kind, but that did not dampen Diana's excitement at finally seeing her name in lights above the cinema in Piccadilly Circus.

Chapter 4

Enter Dennis Hamilton

As a new decade dawned, Diana was contracted out by the Rank Organisation to Ealing Studios to appear in *Dance Hall* (1950). The film, directed by Charles Crichton and produced by Michael Balcon, was to feature rising star Petula Clark and an ensemble cast of young actors. It tells the story of four young women who find respite from the monotony of factory work and their domestic drudgery by spending their evenings dancing at London's Chiswick Palais. There they find romance, glamour and excitement, and experience drama and heartache along the way. The use of the 'portmanteau' style of interwoven stories in itself was not that unusual, but what made *Dance Hall* unique for the time was its focus on female stories and the experiences of young urban women. The screenplay was written by Diana Morgan, alongside Alexander McKendrick and E.V.H. Emmett. It tried to present what was perhaps for the time quite a realistic view of life in urban, working-class Britain with a female perspective, albeit with a rather well-spoken cast.

The film opens with a tracking shot in a real factory introducing the women and setting the context, with noisy machinery combining with the opening title music. These were techniques that would seem at home in the later 1960s British New Wave film canon. *Dance Hall* was filmed on real London streets in Pimlico and south-west London. We see glimpses of London bomb sites and trolleybuses, and there are references to playing the football pools and ration books. The main setting of the film was the familiar dance hall, which was a staple of leisure for the masses at the time. The dance hall was a place for pleasure and enjoyment, an escape from the reality of everyday toil, and gave a sense of community to those trying to find their place in a country recovering from post-war economic and social upheaval. The film is an honest and down-to-earth portrayal of austerity and its effects, and the desire for social mobility it can create.

The film's director, Charles Crichton, is best known for the Ealing comedies such as *Hue and Cry* (1947) and *The Lavender Hill Mob* (1951). Although quite different, *Dance Hall* is a lively film with fast-paced storytelling and excellent use of the dance setting to move things along at pace. There is an excellent supporting cast and the music, provided by Ted Heath and Geraldo who were leaders of the most fashionable big bands of the day, gives it real energy. There is a sense of the burgeoning influence of American popular culture in the film with the occasional jive, but this is still a resolutely British version of how young people spent their leisure time.

Each of the young women bring something different to their own individual story, but each one intertwines, giving it a real episodic feel. There is a love triangle that dominates the main storyline, with Eve (Natasha Parry) trying to decide between the steady and strait-laced Phil (Donald Houston) and handsome American charmer (Bonar Colleano). Eve is quite a liberated young woman for the time, and even listens to jazz music, a worrying sign in conservative 1950s Britain. She makes what seem to be bad choices and the film explores her dilemma. Eve's group of friends includes Georgie, played by Petula Clark, and Mary, played by Jane Hylton. Diana was cast as Carole, who waits around at the Palais, hoping for a dance.

Diana gave a mature performance and her character has an air of all-knowing, slightly jaded cheekiness about her. A raised eyebrow and a knowing look goes a long way to fleshing out the slightness of her storyline. The fresh-faced Petula Clark was actually just a year younger than Diana when they made *Dance Hall*, yet it feels like a gulf of decades on screen. Their experience of being teenagers in showbusiness had been rather different.

Whilst it did not quite achieve the authenticity of later films depicting young lives in flux, *Dance Hall* broke new ground in its effort to tell an identifiable female story of everyday interactions in a natural context and setting. It was not a big hit at the time by Ealing Studios standards, and was often neglected in reflections on the impact of post-war British cinema. But in recent times, it has been revisited and highlighted as a feminist film, which depicts female choices and motives in a changing society, demonstrating its importance in telling working-class female stories in cinema.

However, despite the opportunity it provided for her career, Diana did not enjoy the experience of making it, referring to it rather directly as 'a ghastly film, quite one of the nastiest I have ever made. And, believe me, that's saying something.' She was surprised at the positive reactions she received for her performance, and shocked when years later she saw it playing at a Hollywood cinema with her name in lights above it, referring to it as one her most triumphant films. 'Ah well, that's show business,' was her retort.

Diana's friend Oona continued as her stand-in on *Dance Hall* too. She was still with Patrick, the best friend of Diana's boyfriend. Having endured the struggle of their boyfriends' failed business venture in Dorset, with both young women having to support them financially on their meagre earnings, Oona's fortunes changed when Patrick came into his inheritance. Diana looked forward to the same thing happening for them when Caborn-Waterfield came of age the following year. His brother John was now living with them in the Earls Court flat they shared, and their stepmother gave them a small weekly allowance while they waited to turn 21.

In spring 1950, Diana returned to the theatre and appeared in a production of Charles Macklin's *The Man of the World* in Stratford-upon-Avon, produced by Kenneth Tynan. The play went on to the Arts Theatre in Cambridge, before reaching the Lyric Theatre in Hammersmith. The production also starred Roger Livesey, Ursula Jeans and Lionel Jeffries, who would become a good friend of Diana's for many years to come. Diana enjoyed good reviews for her performance. She recalled, 'I think I surprised many of the people who came to see the play. I think they had wondered what I could do apart from appearing in bad Rank films and posing with Easter bunnies and Christmas balloons for the Rank Publicity Department.' She was even named Actress of the Year by *Theatre World* magazine.

Despite this critical success, her professional life was still rather quiet. She followed her run at the Lyric with an appearance in *Miranda* in Stratford, London, and in the American play *Born Yesterday*, in a small theatre in Henley-on-Thames, an experience that she really enjoyed. That play took up just a week of her time, and the rest of her summer was a blur of parties and good times with her circle of friends. The guest list for parties reads like a *Who's Who* of the young, smart film set of the time. Diana and Caborn-Waterfield also bought a car and they took a holiday in Cornwall. As Diana commented, reflecting on that time, 'At nineteen, to enjoy was the main purpose of every day. This, and to experience everything, regardless of the cost.' But their endless summer skies were soon to be replaced by the black clouds which were looming on the horizon.

Diana was unexpectedly summoned into the head office of the Rank Organisation and told that, due to substantial financial losses, all contract artists were being made redundant immediately. Olive Dodds apparently told her, 'We are not unhappy with your abilities, my dear…but you are not everything that could be expected – least of all, a box-office draw.' Diana could not believe what she was hearing. All her hopes and dreams suddenly came crashing down around her, and she was left in a state of shock. For the years she had been under contract, she had felt safe and secure, knowing that despite not always working, she could draw on her small weekly salary while she waited for the next big opportunity to come dancing round the corner. But now that security had been ripped away from her, leaving her feeling vulnerable. How on earth would she pay her rent?

In an article she wrote for *Picturegoer* magazine in 1950, after being released from her contract, Diana shared her rather candid views on the experience of being affiliated with the Charm School. She demonstrated a mature understanding of its impact on her career potential, 'We were all madly keen and ambitious – and therefore rather frustrated…unless something drastic happened…I was going to be Rank's stock "bad girl"… the flighty, sexy little thing who pops in and out of the story whenever a little light relief seems to be called for.'

On a more positive note, she won a part in a small film, *Worm's Eye View* (1951). Directed by Jack Raymond and starring Ronald Shiner and Garry Marsh, it was set during the Second World War and features a family who let a group of RAF men stay with them, but then find themselves in difficulty with their bitter landlady as a result. Based on the successful play of the same name by R.F. Delderfield, it was a box office success on its release. The role also paid Diana £275, which was a decent rate, but it did not last long when there was nothing else on the horizon. Whilst work was not forthcoming, neither was the support of her so-called friends and acquaintances. They were keen to hang around her when every night was party night, but now they were nowhere to be found and Diana learned a hard lesson in the trappings of fame and success.

Caborn-Waterfield and Diana were fast running out of money and favours. Their last hope was his inheritance. The new year dawned and an envelope from his stepmother arrived, containing birthday wishes and the long-hoped-for inheritance cheque. However, rather than the substantial amount they expected, it contained just £50, the equivalent of less than £2000 in today's money. The accompanying note claimed that business had floundered, wiping out any hope of a fortune. They were devastated as another dream was dashed. As Diana admitted, they soon discovered that there was truth in the saying, 'When poverty comes through the door, love flies out of the window.' They were thrown out of their flat for non-payment of rent, and on a winter's day in early 1951, they gathered up their meagre belongings and prepared themselves to head out into the cold, unsure of where they would end up. As they prepared to leave, Caborn-Waterfield's brother John showed up in dire straits himself, wanting to 'borrow' something worth pawning. They had nothing, of course. He had arrived in a large American convertible, which was still waiting outside for him. Diana asked John who the driver was; she had not seen him before and was intrigued. As he hurried back out of the door and towards the car, he replied that the driver's name was Dennis Hamilton.

For a few months, Diana and her boyfriend drifted through cheap bedsits and the sofas of sympathetic friends. Their relationship centred on borrowing money rather than burning hot passion. They eventually found a bedsit they could just about afford, secured with promises to the owner that they could get him into the movies. Diana felt her career was also going nowhere fast. There was talk of her going to Broadway to appear in Ben Levy's *Springtime for Henry*, but despite the rare feeling of excitement it created for her, it was not to be. Without a job or steady income to keep him on the straight and narrow, Caborn-Waterfield drifted in and out of dubious business deals and dodgy activities, as did his brother John. He and Diana were also drifting apart.

Diana's flailing career did, however, take a turn for the better quite unexpectedly. She was cast in the comedy *Lady Godiva Rides Again*, which was being made at Shepperton Studios and on location in Folkestone. It was not the lead role – that went to a complete unknown, Pauline Stroud – but it was a key role and Diana gave a very assured performance. The film tells the story of a shy, young woman called Marjorie Clark (played by Stroud), who enters a beauty contest in the hope of winning fame and fortune but ends up being cast as Lady Godiva in a nude show. Diana, now sporting blonde hair, plays a rather jaded beauty queen who shows new girl Marjorie the ropes. The film was apparently inspired by the Miss Kent beauty competition in 1950, where Frank Launder, joint producer of the film with Leslie Gilliat, was one of the judges. The film is a bit of an ensemble piece, with a host of known faces making sometimes rather brief appearances, including Stanley Holloway, John McCallum, Dora Bryan and a young Sid James. There are also uncredited appearances by Alastair Sim, Googie Withers and Trevor Howard. It was later re-released to capitalise on Diana's fame, with her role given star billing on the posters.

Diana felt relieved to be working again at last. Caborn-Waterfield, however, ended up in court over yet another dodgy deal. Diana recalled that she accepted a lift back to London with a young co-star and her boyfriend, but just as they were about to leave, the boyfriend told her there was not enough room in the car for her, leaving her high and dry. The boyfriend was Dr Stephen Ward, the influential society osteopath and artist who later found notoriety as a key figure during the Profumo political scandal. He later died of an overdose in 1963 just before the verdict was announced in his subsequent trial for immorality offences.

Back in London and working sporadically at Shepperton on *Lady Godiva Rides Again*, Diana had some free time one afternoon so she visited a club she had been to a few times before. It was the kind of place that attracted a crowd of would-be young stars, and Diana was sat with a friend when a man at the next table leaned over and asked her for a light. She had seen him there before; he was handsome and appeared to be vibrant company to those he mixed with. They got chatting as a group and he was charming, generously offering to pay for everyone's dinner. She was drawn in by his sparkling blue eyes, and when he suggested they go elsewhere, Diana found herself saying yes. As they walked towards his car, a fancy American convertible, she realised he was Dennis Hamilton. He was not her usual type, but she was hooked. As she recalled in her autobiography, 'It was Dennis's personality which really bowled me over…Added to that was a dazzling smile which charmed everyone, regardless of what they thought about him, his motives or his principles. Not that he had any of the latter, as I was to discover.'

That evening, Diana felt it was the beginning of something important. Hamilton was older than her at 26, but they had a lot in common and she referred to it as a 'strange kinship' between them. He knew the movie business, having worked as a stand-in and a bit-part actor in a few films, but despite his handsome looks he had never made a career of acting. Instead he had drifted through various dead-end jobs, shady business deals and wealthy women, and was always a great salesman in every capacity. Diana described him as having a hypnotic effect on everyone who met him, which made them do things they never even knew they wanted to do. She claimed that she never fell in love with Hamilton, or loved him, but instead was caught in the spider's web he created. She felt he was incapable of loving anyone but himself. Theirs was a complex relationship from the start, and it would have a powerful and lasting effect on Diana and her career. She later said, 'I knew less how to handle him at the end than I did at the beginning.'

At this point, Diana was still living with Caborn-Waterfield, who was awaiting his court case. But Hamilton pursued her regardless. From the outset, Diana never really knew where she stood with him. Sometimes he was charm personified, other times he was aloof and cold. When Caborn-Waterfield was given a short prison sentence, Hamilton concentrated all his efforts on winning her over. Red roses, poetry, all effort was made to take advantage of the situation to woo her, and it resulted in a whirlwind romance. Diana had not set out to hurt or betray Caborn-Waterfield as she loved him deeply, but Hamilton stepped into the void created by his absence. When he asked Diana to marry him after just a few short weeks, she said yes.

As she was under 21, Diana had to gain consent from her parents in order to get married. Considering how they had reacted to her engagement to Caborn-Waterfield, she steeled herself for their protestations. However, to her amazement, they agreed to it straight away over the phone, despite never having met Hamilton. The other concern for the couple was an older woman Hamilton had been in a relationship with. He was cited as co-respondent in her divorce, which Diana did not discover until her wedding day. Caborn-Waterfield, who was still in prison, obviously did not take the news of Diana's wedding well, allegedly arranging for a friend to phone the registry office anonymously to suggest her parents' consent had been forged. Ironically, Diana later admitted that it was technically true, because she had forged their signatures as her parents were actually away on holiday when the papers needed to be signed. It was hardly the romantic day she had dreamed of, and Diana inevitably had serious doubts. She still loved Caborn-Waterfield, and had only known Hamilton for five weeks but she was so conflicted.

On the day of their wedding, 3 July 1951, they arrived at Caxton Hall to find a flurry of reporters, photographers and film fans wanting to catch a glimpse of the bride. They hurried inside to be greeted by an official who raised concerns about the consent due to the anonymous phone call. According to Diana, Hamilton reacted angrily, grabbing the man physically. This was to be the first time she witnessed the rage that he could display, turning it on in the blink of an eye. But the situation was resolved and Diana married Hamilton that day in the small registry office. She was 19 years of age. There was no reception planned as the couple had no money. Even her wedding ring had been purchased hastily with borrowed cash, so they celebrated with a meal of spaghetti and wine in a small Italian restaurant. There was no dream honeymoon either. She later said that she assumed all brides felt like she did after the ceremony: nervy and depressed.

Diana recalled that the first few days of marriage were strange. By the end of the first week, they had apparently split up and reconciled twice. She knew deep down that neither of them was actually sure they had done the right thing, but decided it was best to just make the most of it, 'uncertain, penniless and questioning.' She was also apprehensively waiting for Caborn-Waterfield's imminent release from prison, and a potential showdown with her new husband. But when she saw him, there were tears rather than recriminations. Their meeting was, however, interrupted by a furious call from Hamilton demanding she return to him, his icily delivered 'You're my wife now' ringing in her ears as she did so. The consequences of her actions finally dawned on her and Diana realised she was now married to a virtual stranger, 'It was so sickening that I began to hate Dennis almost as much as I hated myself for being so stupid. Nevertheless I went back and tried to make the best of what looked, at that moment, a very bad job!'

Their married life began in an elegant house in Beauchamp Place, Knightsbridge, though Diana had no clue how they could afford the rent on it. She was about to start work on a new film being made at Bray Studios, with the American actor George Brent, star of *The Spiral Staircase* (1946). The film was *The Last Page* (1952), a British noir made by Hammer Films and directed by Terence Fisher, who went on to direct many of Hammer's later horror film successes. As well as Brent, it stars American actress Marguerite Chapman. Brent plays a bookstore manager who is blackmailed by his attractive young employee, played by Diana, and her small-time crook boyfriend after he tries to kiss her. The film was known as *Man Bait* in America, the poster for it featuring a scantily-clad and seductive-looking Diana with the tagline 'Blonde Blackmail!'

The film was made under a deal between Hammer Films and the US film distribution company, Lippert Pictures. Under the deal, a well-known Hollywood actor supplied by Lippert would be cast in the leading role to ensure success with American audiences. The deal lasted a few years and produced a number of successes. But the rather British and pared-back proceedings at the small studio must have been rather a shock to Hollywood star Brent.

Diana was still secretly in touch with Michael Caborn-Waterfield. Feeling guilty about how she had betrayed him, she gave him money so he could go off to France to start again, ironically with another of her lost loves, Anthony Newley. Caborn-Waterfield and his failed business deals had often been the bane of their relationship, and he was always into something. Eventually he would go on to found the successful lingerie and sex toy brand, Ann Summers, in 1970, by opening its first sex shop, which he named after his secretary. He sold the company the following year to brothers David and Ralph Gold, and with David's daughter, Jacqueline Gold, at the helm, they turned it into a successful business empire. Caborn-Waterfield led a distinctly chequered life after his time with Diana, including smuggling guns into Cuba and serving time in a French prison. One report after his death aged 86 in 2016 reflected, 'He actually possessed few redeeming features although he had an ability to charm which he put to good use.' *The Times* newspaper reported, 'He was not known to conform to the high ethical standards that most people take for granted, and indeed had several brushes with the law during his life... Throughout it, he inspired love from many beautiful – preferably rich – women, some of whom were considerably younger than him. He divested them of their clothes and sometimes their fortunes.'

When Hamilton discovered that Diana had been giving money to Caborn-Waterfield, he apparently flew into an angry, violent rage. Diana recalls in her autobiography that he hit her and called her a whore, before calling her parents in the middle of the night to tell them of her treachery. Yet again she was shocked by how quickly the man she had hastily married could change. 'He drove himself on a tireless wave of dangerous, exciting emotion,' was how Diana referred to him, despite the fact she also admitted that he terrified her. At just 19, Diana was perhaps too young to fully understand the dangerous situation she was in. He watched her every move, paranoid that every man she met would make a move on her and that she would comply. After a day's filming, he would demand to know every interaction she had and every conversation.

When an American producer offered her a Hollywood contract, he stipulated that she should divorce Hamilton. He claimed that he could not make her a star if she was married. Naturally the suggestion did not go down well with her husband. Diana concluded filming on *The Last Page* at Bray Studios, with hardly a penny of the money she earned left after she had apparently given most of it to Caborn-Waterfield. Hamilton was also broke after his business folded. Their rent was overdue, his beloved car was repossessed and the bailiffs were at the door. He insisted they should move out of London. Diana was appalled by the idea, thinking the countryside would leave her feeling bereft of all the luxuries and activities she was used to. But move they did, putting their belongings in the back of a borrowed car and driving out to rural Surrey.

Diana felt depressed at the state of her floundering film career. There was no Hollywood contract like she had dreamed of, and no consistent domestic work to keep her energised. She felt like a failure. But Hamilton had started taking an interest in her career and was determined that he would make her a star. His angle would be to make her the 'female Errol Flynn, always in trouble'. It would be all about the publicity he could generate. His first idea was to claim to the press that Diana had turned down a Hollywood contract to stay in the UK and make films in the country she loved. The press loved it. And so began a relationship with the press that would come to dominate her life and career: the craving of publicity. Diana later said that Hamilton assumed the role of her Svengali, a 'star creator', and that it would lead to the breakdown of their marriage and damage her career: 'Like everything else he did, Dennis's greatest fault was never knowing when to stop.'

Although things were quiet at first, Diana finally had some positive work news. The BBC called, offering her a role on a TV show with Terry-Thomas. Already a successful comedian and character actor at the time, Terry-Thomas went on to have a long and fruitful film career in the 1950s and 1960s, often portraying rather disreputable members of the upper classes, the cads, toffs and bounders.

The show Diana was offered, *How Do You View?*, was broadcast live and is referred to as the first comedy programme on British television. First broadcast in 1949 and running for five series until 1953, the programme utilised Terry-Thomas's well-known mischievous persona and included a series of sketches in which he appeared with a number of guest stars playing regular characters, including Diana. Ground-breaking in many ways, the show made much of its 'live television' status, and featured Thomas walking through the television studio and the corridors of the BBC. Diana remembered Terry-Thomas fondly. They remained good friends, and he went on to become godfather to Diana's second son Gary.

Hamilton drove her to rehearsals in London every day and waited for her to finish. He did the same whenever she had a meeting with a potential producer or discussion about a role. Sometimes Diana got the impression that these conversations might lead somewhere if she played the usual game expected of female stars. The suggestion of sex was often subtle, sometimes more overt, but it had been a part of the scene since her early teens, and nothing had changed on that front. Diana was always paranoid about Hamilton now anyway and how he would react, despite his own sexual conduct. Sex was a large part of his personal life, and not necessarily with his wife. She strongly suspected him of cheating on her, and later learned of his infidelities, which apparently even occurred when she was at home. He and his close friend Jimmy Mellon were known to arrange orgies, in order to spy on proceedings as voyeurs, by hiding in cupboards or behind mirrors. Diana recalled that she was rather bemused by it all and a little disgusted. As time moved on, Hamilton would apparently plant tape recorders in people's bedrooms and make spyholes in walls, claiming it was all just a silly practical joke if he was caught, with Diana admitting she would go along with the laughter. She was also aware of his interest in screening sex films, some professional and some homemade through secret filming, in their private cinema for a selected audience of young girls, although she claimed that she stumbled across this information by accident.

Hamilton had a special two-way mirror fitted in their Chelsea home, apparently without Diana knowing, hidden under the floorboards. Below was the guest room. Diana admits in her first autobiography, written in 1960 and just a few years after her relationship with Hamilton ended, that she knew of sexual activities taking place in their home during their regular house parties. Usually these parties were attended by couples, with 'starstruck' young women also present, who were encouraged to have sex in the guest room by men posing as film producers. Apparently unbeknown to the young women, and also to Diana herself according to her account, the other guests would be watching from above. However, this account is slightly at odds with those of friends who attended these types of parties, particularly male friends who were apparently cajoled and seduced by young women attending, and encouraged into the bedroom to take things further, unaware of the audience behind the mirror.

Later she admitted to becoming rather blasé about it all, 'I gradually came to look upon conduct that would shock a London typist as quite normal. I know better now.' But she always seemed to qualify any comments about those times as her being under Hamilton's influence. According to friends, however, she was always part of the proceedings as hostess, making sure guests were happy, filling their glasses and milling around, happy to be the one to make sure they were enjoying themselves. She never drank herself, however, always keeping a clear head. Her good memory made for publicity gold in later years.

Diana endured her time living in the Surrey countryside, awaiting her next work opportunity. They made few friends around the area, and their lack of funds often led to Hamilton pulling a fast one with local tradespeople, or making dodgy deals with shops to ensure they ate above and beyond their rations. But their errant behaviour eventually caught up with the Hamiltons and they had to cut their ties with Dunsfold and move on again. It was around this time that Diana discovered she was pregnant again. Despite being married, Hamilton was having none of it. A baby was not on the list of things he wanted. He thought having a child would just be an obstacle on Diana's path to fame and fortune. He quickly arranged for her to see a doctor who would perform an abortion. This time it cost considerably more and would not be carried out on a kitchen table.

They left Dunsfold under cover of night, their belongings bulging out of the back of their less-than-showbiz-friendly Opel car. Their young Labrador puppy, Topaz, accompanied them, a present from Hamilton to Diana. A puppy was allowed, but a baby was not. Their next home was in Esher, Surrey. It was attractively furnished and at least it was nearer to London, which was a small win for Diana. But there was her abortion to be sorted out and paid for. Having experienced it before, Diana was terrified at the prospect but on a cold morning in February, Hamilton drove her into London to the doctor's private residence. Diana recalled that she felt an indescribable feeling of depression afterwards. Where Hamilton was concerned, life had to continue and Diana was caught up in his usual wave of parties and people, of schemes and laughs. There were always plenty of friends and acquaintances around to distract her.

In an upturn in her professional prospects, one morning Diana received a phone call from a theatre producer, wanting to talk to her about a revue he was staging at the Comedy Theatre in London. They jumped in the car to London, and as they passed a car showroom with a Rolls-Royce for sale, Hamilton, with his usual instinctive reactions, declared that they were going to buy it. Without a penny to their names, he somehow managed to do so and they arrived for their meeting in London in the large black Rolls-Royce instead of the beat-up old Opel. Hamilton had an unwavering belief that she would be cast in the show because now she had a Rolls-Royce to pull up outside the theatre in every night 'just like a star should'. Diana recounted that Hamilton planned to use it as a publicity stunt, announcing that at the age of 20 she was the youngest owner of a Rolls-Royce in the country. Any doubts she had flew out of the window when her fee increased after arriving at the theatre in her fancy car.

The show, *Rendezvous*, was a brilliant success when it opened in Brighton before its transfer to the West End. The audiences loved Diana's performance, as did theatre critics after starting its London run. 'London was at my feet and I was tasting the fruits of success for the first time in my life,' she later said. Whilst the revue show utilised some of Diana's best-known features, such as songs delivered wearing a bikini or dressed in a gymslip, it also served to demonstrate her singing talent and fine sense of comedy. It was an excellent step in her career, and offers of shows and cabaret followed as a result – even a Blackpool summer season was touted.

For once, Diana was faced with having to choose between prospective roles once the show came to an end. One variety agent suggested she tour the music halls to widen her audience base because West End success was soon forgotten and 'you can't eat press cuttings'. After she politely declined, he apparently said that the offer was always open, 'Get a cabaret act under your belt and you'll never go hungry again.' After the flurry of offers, Diana accepted a small role in a film, *My Wife's Lodger*, and the well-paid Blackpool summer season appearing in the show *Life with the Lyons*. Apparently, she had been very keen on a film opportunity with Sir Laurence Olivier, *The Beggar's Opera* (1953), but turned it down in favour of the ready money of Blackpool.

My Wife's Lodger (1952), a comedy directed by Maurice Elvey and starring Dominic Roche, Olive Sloane and Leslie Dwyer, concerns a soldier who returns home after the Second World War, only to find a spiv has become a lodger and very much established himself in his place. A classic tale of a dysfunctional family, the film was based on a play of the same title written by Roche himself. Diana plays a small role but the film has an ensemble feel, playing on its broad appeal and music hall-style comedy. It had a tone and sense of setting that would be utilised by many British television sitcoms in future decades.

After filming concluded, Diana headed north with Hamilton, Topaz the dog and a new poodle called BaBa. Diana found Blackpool to be 'a gusty place', and was not impressed by the prospect of two shows a night for three months. The £100 a week fee made up for it though and she soldiered on. Hamilton was in his element, teaching himself how to be a Svengali. He met with producers and the like, finding out what other stars earned and returning to report to Diana with pound signs in his eyes. Diana had her suspicions that he was also schmoozing the local ladies too. And then there was Hamilton's beloved publicity drive, which was now in full operation. While in Blackpool, Diana experienced her first negative headlines, a story about her being sued by a former landlord. As she was under 21, the judge referred to her as an infant in need of protection, which delighted the newspapers. Hamilton revelled in the situation because his wish to turn her into a 'female Errol Flynn', who was always in trouble and mischief, was coming to fruition. He wanted her to be a 'character' rather than a 'dreary girl next door'. Diana was not keen on the idea herself.

His next move was to turn Diana into a 'wealthy, magical myth' by announcing that she had bought herself an aeroplane and was taking flying lessons. Diana admitted that it was 'flamboyant, colourful stuff' that placed her in a different category from other actresses of the time, the dreamy starlet or the girl-next-door types. It certainly made her stand out. For the premiere of *My Wife's Lodger* in Southport, Hamilton decided they should arrive by plane, apparently piloted by Diana herself. 'What a gimmick if we flew there in our own plane…you'd go down in history as the only film star ever to fly herself to her own premiere,' Hamilton apparently said. Diana was unhappy with the idea but reluctantly went along with it. They took a pilot to fly them and when they landed, Diana emerged from the pilot seat in her glamorous gown for the waiting press, fooling everyone but herself.

Thankfully for Diana, it was soon time to leave Blackpool for the south again. The couple moved back to London, securing a small rented house in Chelsea. At last, she was back in her adopted home city, much to her delight.

Chapter 5

The Face of 1950s British Cinema

As 1952 progressed, Diana's film career was starting to gain some momentum. The two film genres which dominated the British box office in the 1950s were, perhaps inevitably, war films and comedies. The latter category would come to dominate much of her work in that decade. She began work on *The Great Game* (1953), a broad sports-themed comedy based on a play by Basil Thomas, directed by Maurice Elvey and starring James Hayter and Thora Hird. The plot revolves around the chairman of a top-flight English football club who makes an illegal approach to a rising star of a rival club. When his antics are discovered by the football authorities, the chairman becomes embroiled in scandal. Many of the scenes were shot at Brentford F.C.'s ground at Griffin Park, and a number of professional football players appeared in the film. Diana plays to type as what was described by one later film critic as a 'sexpot secretary'. She also had a small role, again as an attractive distraction, in *The Saint's Return* (1953), a British crime thriller featuring the character Simon Templar (The Saint), played by Louis Hayward. The film saw a revival of the fictional detective after a long gap, as the original RKO Pictures series of films ran between 1938 and 1943, also starring Hayward. The character of *The Saint* would be revisited again on television in the 1960s, this time famously portrayed by Roger Moore. Diana appeared briefly in the film, credited as 'The Blonde in Lennar's Apartment'.

Diana's marriage to Hamilton was troubling. He was dominant and controlling, he cheated on her with other women and his violent tantrums scared her. She felt stifled and had a continuing desire to run away, but also felt she needed him, 'I was like a bird in a gilded cage; spoilt, cosseted and cared for in every way, treated like a child who must be sheltered from outside worries and responsibilities. I came to rely on him for everything.' She turned 21 during rehearsals for the play *Remains to Be Seen* in the

West End. Hamilton threw her a huge party, but all the balloons and revelry could not disguise her underlying fears about his behaviour. Yet he continued to watch her every move, hanging around the theatre every evening as she performed. The play was not a success. It opened to lukewarm reviews and closed after just five days.

Feeling disconsolate and unsure what to do next, her new agents suggested she should develop her variety act. She did not think of herself as a variety artist at all, wondering what 'act' she could possibly offer to audiences. However, Hamilton was keen on the idea, especially the fees it could garner. Needing money, and with no other work seemingly forthcoming, Diana agreed. She accepted a five-week tour of variety theatres across the country, including the notorious Glasgow Empire. Her agents organised for an act to be written for her, including lines, music and lyrics. She inevitably bombed in Glasgow, 'For three nights I battled with audiences who mercifully did not throw things or give me the bird but whose silence proved that I was not the star attraction I was made out to be.' But the money was still good, much to the delight of Hamilton and her agents.

When she was handed her cut of the money at the end of the disastrous Glasgow run, she felt a strange mix of guilt and excitement. She was performing at her worst, yet earning more comparably than she had before. It did not feel right, but the words of an agent 'You can't eat press cuttings' echoed through her mind. She fared better in Brighton, Portsmouth and Hull but despite Hamilton being delighted with 'their' earnings, she hated it. She wanted to be acting in front of the film cameras. But after the disappointment of the first variety tour, she set about working on her material and refining her act until it felt more comfortable. She took on more variety dates and felt she fared better the second time around, which gave her confidence.

Hamilton was still enjoying his assumed status as her Svengali, taking pleasure in fooling the press with his stunts, but also more worryingly decreeing himself as the secret of her success. He seemed to control her every move; 'Dors would not get from here to the garden gate without me,' he would apparently boast. He continued to watch her every move, never letting her out of his sight. He apparently opened her mail, intercepted phone calls and discouraged her friends. It felt to Diana like she was in prison, 'He thought for me, about me and around me.' She wanted to end the marriage, but felt she was trapped in a spider's web. All the time he was jealously and possessively guarding her against attention from other men. He, on the other hand, was seeing other women to stoke his ego, always wanting to prove to himself that they found him fascinating.

Hamilton decided to use her hard-earned cash to secure a mortgage on a bigger house and, as Diana toured more theatres with her variety act, he set about decorating. He also said yes to a photographer who had an idea for a booklet, *Diana Dors in 3D*, which would contain a series of risqué photographs of Diana in skimpy clothing and draped in furs. 'I posed in innumerable positions and semi-nude drapes with wispy bits of white fur,' she later said. The booklet proved to be a huge success and generated great publicity, but unfortunately the couple had accepted a modest one-off fee rather than a percentage. It was later denounced as 'obscene' by magistrates in Halifax.

Hamilton was creating quite a publicity machine for Diana, with gimmicks like the Rolls-Royce and similar stunts, and claims appearing in the tabloids to keep her name in the public consciousness. He played up her wealth and success, which later even prompted questions from MPs in parliament about how at odds with austerity Britain it was. One MP asked why actors could have so much money when the ordinary man in the street could not, even suggesting Diana was earning more than a cabinet minister. The newspapers went to town yet again when her name was mentioned in parliament. It also brought unwanted interest from the taxman. Diana was always keen afterwards to point out that such sums of money and riches never existed, and that it was just Hamilton drumming up publicity to bolster her film star image.

Hamilton's idea was to market Diana as 'Britain's Marilyn Monroe', a blonde bombshell who could compete with the Hollywood star. It raised her profile, certainly, but she was not securing the big film roles to justify it in her mind. Diana would come to resent the label imposed on her, as it was one she could never really shake off, 'How many times…had I been tagged as the British answer to someone or other!' she lamented. Yet while Monroe was given the chance to appear in star-studded successes like *Gentlemen Prefer Blondes* and *How to Marry a Millionaire*, Diana felt the rather less grand titles she was being offered simply would not cut it.

Diana started work on another film, *Is Your Honeymoon Really Necessary?* (1953), a light comedy romp directed by Maurice Elvey and based on Vivian Tidmarsh's hit West End play of the same name. Elvey has the accolade of being the most prolific British film director, with over 200 titles to his name. Diana plays a mischievous first wife trying to disrupt her ex's new marriage. The ex-husband is played by Diana's acquaintance, Bonar Colleano, whom Hamilton thought was a complete ladies' man. Colleano was later killed, aged just 34, when he crashed his sports car returning home when working in Liverpool. His then wife, Susan Shaw, a fellow attendee of the Rank Charm School whom Diana worked with a number of times, fell into alcoholism after her husband's death and her acting career never recovered. Shaw's funeral in 1978 was apparently paid for by the Rank Organisation.

Diana then headed to Manchester to work on a film with northern comedian and ex-music hall star, Frank Randle. The rather unusual film, *It's a Grand Life* (1953), is set in the army, telling the story of life in the Essex Regiment after the Second World War. Randle plays an army private and the film focuses on his various escapades. Diana appears as Paula Clements, a young corporal in the Women's Royal Army Corps being pursued and harassed by her lusty male boss, with Randle coming to the rescue for the object of his affections. The film is more a set of comedy sketches than a normal narrative, and later critics haven't been kind, with Tony Sloman commenting, 'Randle has neither the wit of George Formby nor the warmth of Gracie Fields, and by the time this movie was made he was looking tired and rather grubby.' The age gap between Randle and Diana seems rather inappropriate to modern audiences, and the humour is quite vulgar and parochial even at the time of its release.

Diana described the experience of working on *It's a Grand Life* as a complete shambles, with Randle, who owned the production company, allegedly drunk for most of the shoot. On one particular day, Randle failed to show up at all so Diana and Hamilton headed to Blackpool to meet up with some friends. But a boozy practical joke went wrong, and Diana, Hamilton and another friend ended up being arrested by police for housebreaking. They were charged and had to appear in court, and although Diana was given an absolute discharge for it being her first offence, the incident generated a barrage of publicity.

Instead of fearing for the effect on Diana's serious acting career, Hamilton thought it was brilliant. He was turning her into the 'female Errol Flynn' after all. And the following evening when she walked on stage at her next variety gig, the house was packed, thanks to the bonus publicity. She began her act with a quip, 'It was a bit of a job getting those handcuffs off but I made it,' to glorious applause. But the scandal upset her parents, and Diana, of course. The newspapers went to town with salacious headlines and revelled in her infamy. Hamilton loved it – that sort of widespread coverage could not be bought. He would later also go to town on making sure she was seen to have an extravagant lifestyle to match her film star persona, decorating their home in lavish and expensive style, and making sure the press were invited in to see it in all its glory. The tax man was also paying attention too, which would later come to haunt her. The publicity machine kept on working.

Ironically, her next film role after the court incident involved a bit of prison time. Social drama *The Weak and the Wicked* (1954), directed by J. Lee Thompson and starring Glynis Johns, was set in a women's prison and filmed at Elstree Studios. Part melodrama, part social realism, the film takes a sympathetic approach to the subject, tracking inmates through their imprisonment and subsequent return to society. With a large cast, the female prisoners talk about the events that brought them there and each of their stories is detailed in a series of flashbacks. While some are successfully rehabilitated, some are not and follow a different path. The film includes the stories of upper-class Jean (Johns) and pregnant Pat, played by Rachel Roberts. Diana was cast as a young inmate, the brassy Betty, who is led astray. The screenwriter and author of the original book, Joan Henry, had herself served time in prison. The film has a feel of authenticity about the prison experience for women in that period. Henry was also working on another idea at the time, about a woman's experience awaiting the death sentence for murder. She was developing the idea with director Thompson, whom she later married, and commented that she and Thompson had discussed Diana for the lead role. Diana felt cautiously excited at the prospect of a rare opportunity in a leading role. That film project would later become *Yield to the Night*.

After filming wrapped on *The Weak and the Wicked*, Diana was asked to do a long-running radio series entitled *Calling All Forces*. The young comedy writer and performer, Bob Monkhouse, and his writing partner, Dennis Goodwin, were involved with the series. Aimed at 'our boys' in uniform around the world, *Calling All Forces* was a massive hit with audiences. The young writers, aged just 22 and 21 respectively, were nicknamed 'radio's young masters of mirth' by one newspaper, and the show was broadcast to millions. It made their comedy careers. There were plenty of guest stars, but when Monkhouse found out about the star of this particular show, he was delighted.

He and Goodwin arrived for Saturday rehearsals at the Playhouse Theatre on Northumberland Avenue as usual. Diana arrived bang on time, sending the assembled men of the production into a flap. Monkhouse greeted her as she made her entrance into the room. In his 1993 autobiography, *Crying with Laughter*, Monkhouse said, 'She was the vibrant incarnation of every Hollywood fantasy of my adolescence and I was dumbstruck.' The first thing she did was compliment his writing. Rehearsals went swimmingly, Diana delighting the musicians and cast with her quick wit and professionalism, her delivery of the script and comic timing often tinged with a cheeky double entendre. She was in her element.

The recording of the show in front of the live audience later that afternoon was apparently rather eventful. Inevitably, the presence of Diana Dors had a massive effect on the audience of male service personnel, building them up into near frenzy. Every line she delivered was met with delighted cheers and applause. It went so well that the live show started to overrun, so the writers had to cut lines and re-write on the hoof. The final sketch, a parody of the 1942 Hedy Lamarr film *White Cargo*, which Diana played with comedians Max Wall and Ted Ray, almost ended in disaster due to a mix-up over the hastily cut dialogue. Diana ended up delivering a line which was so heavy in implied sexual connotations, the audience could barely contain themselves. The listeners at home must have wondered what on earth was happening. The fact they started ringing the BBC switchboards to find out made the show's bosses see red the next day, and the young writers were put on probation as a result of the furore. But the listening figures told a different story. The episode had been massively popular, and Diana was booked to appear again. In fact, she appeared many times, becoming a staple feature of the show.

Diana described being immediately and enormously attracted to Monkhouse, his humour and intelligence winning her over from the start. She was particularly vulnerable to his sensitive charms given her tumultuous relationship with her husband. Diana felt that the attraction was mutual. It certainly was, as Monkhouse himself later admitted that he had been a big fan of Diana's even before they met. He recalled, 'It was her energy that first attracted me,' after he saw her years previously in *Penny and the Pownall Case*. 'Her acting was raw but promising and her vitality made me remember her afterwards as if her part of the screen had been in colour.' He followed her career as she became everyone's favourite blonde pin-up girl, commenting that she gave the camera the same amused gaze that he came to discover she gave everything in life. When they met at that first recording, despite both being married to other people, they immediately liked each other, developing feelings of affection that lasted for thirty years. Diana later said of Monkhouse, 'I was 20 and married but I fell madly in love with him. It was not just the way he looked that appealed to me, but his intelligence and wit.'

They spent a lot of time together, particularly on the days of the show's rehearsals and recordings, which would last a number of hours. After several shows recorded in London, the programme was deemed to be flagging a bit by the bosses, so to inject a bit of life into it, they sent it on the road. First stop, Germany. They were dispatched to the forces base in Hamburg to boost the morale of the tired personnel stationed out there. An evening with Diana Dors was just the tonic they needed. On the overnight ferry voyage to the Netherlands to start the train journey into Germany, Diana was the only person not to be seasick. On arrival in Hamburg, she reportedly enjoyed the shopping so much, she filled three empty suitcases with fancy clothes and underwear, all frivolities not available in heavily-rationed Britain.

The show recordings were a huge success. After each one, the cast put on a concert for the audience. Monkhouse recalled how radiant Diana looked in her outfits, and how beautifully she sang. Her voice was a revelation to everyone and he thought her enchanting. Singing a number of songs, including 'I Wanna be Loved by You', made famous by Marilyn Monroe, she wowed the crowds, and Monkhouse. He commented that when she came off stage, the crowd's huge applause still going, she kissed him a thank you and he felt like proposing. It was a magical end to the show.

His fondness for Diana continued, and Monkhouse admitted that he even attended one of the Hamiltons' famous parties in 1952 when his wife was away visiting family, giving a rather eye-opening account of the experience in his own autobiography. In the summer of 1953 they worked together again, and their mutual attraction would cause even more trouble. They were both appearing in a radio variety show recorded at the Scala Theatre in London. There were a number of well-known comedy and variety stars involved with the show, including Tony Hancock, Irene Handl and Benny Hill. Diana had been brought in as one of two 'leading ladies': a sweet English rose-type was filled by musical star Lizbeth Webb, and Diana was there as the 'sexy bombshell sort of piece', as the producer elegantly put it.

But spending so much time together again re-ignited the spark between them. They joked around together and tried hard to hide the simmering passion they obviously felt for each other, which was becoming noticeable to those working with them. Their juvenile antics masked a very serious situation that they tried to fight. But Hamilton had his suspicions, angrily accusing Diana of having an affair with Monkhouse (if only! thought Diana). He would collect her from the theatre, cutting a very menacing figure and greeting Monkhouse with overt resentment. Despite Monkhouse's efforts, for weeks they never had the chance to be alone for him to make a move.

Eventually, according to Monkhouse, they did finally consummate their passion for each other, spending one night together in a borrowed apartment after much manoeuvring on both sides to make it happen, and the rather random intervention of comedian Charlie Chester. It was an afternoon that Monkhouse said he never forgot. It was never to be for the two of them, however, and they had to make do with wistful smiles and looks of yearning from then on.

Diana knew that despite her feelings for him, there was no future for her and Monkhouse. She thought they would have made a great team too. There was also the big issue of Hamilton and his suspicions about their relationship. For the rest of the recordings of the variety series, he hung around all day, watching her every move. Monkhouse knew about Dennis Hamilton's reputation for violence, and he feared the reprisals if he ever found out about their liaison. It was a fear that never really went away while Hamilton was still on the scene.

At a party later on, one particularly frightening encounter with Hamilton scared Monkhouse, making him fear for his life after apparent threats to kill were made by Hamilton at the time. In a panic at seeing him unexpectedly, Monkhouse even felt compelled to inflict his own physical retaliation on Hamilton at another party a few years later. He never could shake the thought that Hamilton might do away with him for sleeping with his wife. But despite that shadow hanging over them, Diana and Monkhouse kept in touch over the years, cementing their fondness for each other into a lasting friendship. Diana described their friendship as, 'A pretty "milk and water end" description of what I figured then was the Romeo and Juliet affair of the decade,' and joking that they both thought they might eventually end up together when they were very old, and too old to do anything about it.

As 1954 started, Diana was again slogging away with her variety act at regional theatres around the country, with Hamilton in tow to make sure she behaved herself. She described feeling like a trapped butterfly, able to spread her wings momentarily before being put away again in her little box.

There was to be good news on the film front, however, as she was being considered for a lead role in Carol Reed's *A Kid For Two Farthings* (1955), scripted by Wolf Mankowitz from his 1953 novel of the same name, based on his experience of growing up in the Jewish community in the East End of London. She was amongst a number of names being put forward and her confidence was low given some of her recent disappointments. But she was elated when she received the call to say the part was hers, 'The name of Dors was about to streak like a meteor through the skies, and cause people in filmland really to sit up and take notice of it.'

Reed was an acclaimed and well-respected director, starting his career at Ealing Studios and Gainsborough in the 1930s, with films such as *Laburnum Grove* (1936), *Bank Holiday* (1938) and *The Stars Look Down* (1939). By the 1940s he was gaining in status and considered to be one of the best directors of his generation. He made *Odd Man Out* in 1947, and then directed two incredibly successful Graham Greene adaptations, *The Fallen Idol* (1948) and perhaps his masterpiece, *The Third Man* (1949) starring Orson Welles in a breath-taking performance. Reed would go on to collaborate again with Greene on *Our Man in Havana* (1960) and at the end of that decade, he surprised everyone with his first and only musical, the much-loved Lionel Bart adaptation of Oliver Twist, *Oliver!* (1968) for which he won an Oscar for Best Director.

A Kid for Two Farthings was Reed's first film made in colour. It tells the story of Joe, played by Jonathan Ashmore, a young boy living with his mother in the working-class Jewish neighbourhood of the East End. His mother Joanna (played by Celia Johnson) works for a tailor, Mr Kandinsky (David Kossoff), and they live right in the heart of the bustling community. Joe wants to help his neighbours, and when he overhears Mr Kandinsky saying a unicorn will grant any wish you ask of it, he sets about trying to find one. What he finds is a poorly young goat with one horn, and he becomes determined to look after it, thinking it will be the answer to everyone's problems.

Diana plays Sonia, a local girl pursuing a romance with her bodybuilder boyfriend, Sam (Joe Robinson). She wants to settle down and get married, and fantasises about the lovely home they could have together, but they have been engaged for four years with seemingly no hope of finding the money to do so. Wanting to earn enough to buy Sonia an actual engagement ring and make things more permanent, Sam gets involved with a dodgy local wrestling promoter, landing him, Sonia and young Joe in trouble.

Filmed partially on Petticoat Lane, which at the time was still at the heart of the East End Jewish community, *A Kid for Two Farthings* boasts a cast of character actors including Irene Handl and Sid James. It is a rather sentimental film but with real heart, a tale of hope amongst hardship told through a whimsical story, rather than the gritty realism of films that followed later in the decade. Whilst the film sometimes feels over the top, Diana gave an acclaimed performance, bringing humour and realism to the part of Sonia, and showing what an assured and natural performer she was, even when the material she was given perhaps was not consistently top quality. She described working on the film as a sheer joy. She was impressed by the professionalism of everyone involved, and the quiet and ordered atmosphere on set was a wonderful contrast to her chaotic experiences of filming previously. She also loved working with Reed.

During filming, Diana and Hamilton sold their London home and moved to Bray in Berkshire. Despite the previous disappointing experience of living in the countryside, Diana's apprehension was wiped out when she saw the new house and its riverside setting. Tranquil, and away from the noise and distractions of London, it felt like a home. At first it proved to be a very happy period for Diana, because she felt settled for the first time, her film career was flourishing, and they had money for once. However, despite her happiness at home, she was still subject to negative publicity.

What followed was one of Diana's most successful years in her film career. 1955 began with a role in *Value for Money* for the Rank Organisation. Directed by Ken Annakin and also starring John Gregson, Susan Stephen and Derek Farr, the light-hearted comedy film tells the story of Chayley Broadbent, a wealthy young man from Yorkshire (played by Gregson), who has inherited his father's rag business. He has also inherited his father's cautiousness with money, much to the annoyance of his fiancée Ethel (Stephen) who will not marry him until he learns how to enjoy himself a bit more. On a visit to London, Chayley goes to a nightclub and meets stunning stage dancer Ruthine, played by Diana. He is so enamoured, he proposes to her as well. Ruthine decides to take him for every penny he is worth, and he chooses to let her.

Diana gives a spirited performance. It is a lightweight comedy and she demonstrates her ability to deliver her lines with the necessary wit and whimsy, playing Ruthine as more than just a pretty face. There is a nice screen relationship between her and Stephen as her love rival, Ethel, as they build an unlikely camaraderie. *Value for Money* was filmed on location in Batley, West Yorkshire, including scenes in the market square, the cemetery and Wilton Park. It was the second film Diana made on location in Yorkshire, the first being *A Boy, a Girl and a Bike* in 1949. Despite her own best efforts to add a bit of depth to her character, *Value for Money* exploits Diana's overt sexuality as Ruthine. As Sue Harper and Vincent Porter suggest in *British Cinema of the 1950s*, 'She strikes sexual terror into the heart of the innocent manufacturer Chayley…and fleeces him royally.'

Despite dropping her a few years previously, the Rank Organisation was now chasing her to sign another contract with them, this time on star terms. Negotiations, which Diana suggested were swayed by Dennis's shrewd talking, resulted in a profitable £7,000 a year deal with an obligation to only make one film for Rank. Quite an achievement, and a reflection of her increasing value as an artist. She also filmed another comedy, *An Alligator Named Daisy* (1955) with director J. Lee Thompson, who she would go on to work with in *Yield to the Night* later that year. *An Alligator Named Daisy* also stars Donald Sinden, Jeannie Carson and James Robertson Justice. It tells the story of Peter Weston, a rather unsuccessful London songwriter played by Sindon, who on returning from a cricket match in Ireland by ferry, is left lumbered with an alligator abandoned by a fellow passenger. He is caught trying to offload his new acquisition overboard by fellow passenger Moira (Carson), who happens to work at London Zoo. She insists he treat Daisy the alligator humanely. They bond and decide to travel back to London together. They are, however, both apparently engaged to other people. Weston is betrothed to Vanessa, the daughter of a wealthy newspaper magnate, played by Diana. Chaos ensues as Peter tries to hide Daisy the alligator from his family whilst trying to find a home for her in various places, culminating in a rather dramatic and very public finale as Peter has to decide what he really wants.

The rather implausible plot makes for a pleasantly charming musical comedy, although Diana again had to do a lot with an underwritten role. Often, she is on screen to seemingly show off her pretty costumes and attractive figure, rather than be allowed by the script to display her acting talent. Many well-known images of Diana are taken from the film and publicity around it. *An Alligator Named Daisy* is an unusual film, given the inclusion of several songs. It is not a pure musical, more a tuneful farce. But that perhaps just adds to the very British charm of it. As with many films of its time, it is bolstered by an impressive and talented supporting cast, including a brief cameo from Margaret Rutherford.

Diana made another film directed by Thompson that year, *As Long as They're Happy* (1955). Another frothy musical comedy made in colour, it stars Jack Buchanan, Janette Scott and Susan Stephen. Buchanan plays a stockbroker, who somehow ends up having a famous American singer to stay in his house, much to the delight of his three daughters, one of whom falls madly in love with him. Diana has a smaller role as an actress and party girl who sings 'The Hokey Pokey Polka'. Again, the role capitalises on Diana's physical allure rather than her acting ability.

The year also saw the release of *Miss Tulip Stays the Night* (1955), a comedy crime caper directed by Leslie Arliss and also starring Patrick Holt, Jack Hulbert and Cicely Courtneidge. Diana stars as Kate Dax, the wife of a crime writer, played by Holt. When the couple stay at a country house, a mysterious corpse appears. It is not exactly one of Diana's favourite films, and one publication referred to it as 'badly done on all counts.'

Despite the professional successes Diana enjoyed, the year was also marked by personal tragedy and difficulties. Diana caught Hamilton with another woman; she suspected that she was just one of many he was seeing behind her back but when she confronted her husband with the evidence, he reacted angrily. They had a terrible fight and he apparently hit her in the face. As she reflected, it was just another nail in the coffin of their troubled marriage. This was nothing compared to the emotional trauma that was to follow, as a few weeks later, Diana's mother Mary suffered a heart attack after an operation and died. Diana was distraught, especially as they had not been as close in recent years, 'It was as if a dagger had been plunged into my heart.'

Later that year, she also discovered she was pregnant again. Despite being in a better financial position than when she had fallen pregnant a few years previously, Hamilton still opposed the idea of starting a family. He had always responded with, 'There's plenty of time for that, Dors, when you're older' when they had discussed children. He apparently wavered this time, but then announced, 'No babies for us yet, there's too much to lose Dors,' and that was that: Diana had another abortion.

She threw herself into her film work while Hamilton worked on his latest business venture: opening a coffee bar in Maidenhead. That summer, Diana headed to the Venice Film Festival along with other Rank stars. Instead of arriving with her fellow Rank actors, however, Hamilton insisted that she turn up separately in a powder-blue Cadillac convertible to grab press attention. This stunt paled into insignificance, however, when she travelled down the Grand Canal wearing a mink bikini. Naturally, the assembled press photographers went wild for her, and the pictures were splashed across the papers all over the world. The incident was later made into a 1956 London stage musical called *Grab Me a Gondola* by James Gilbert and Julien More, in which a reporter covers the antics of a young film starlet at the Venice Film Festival. It ran for nearly 700 performances at the Lyric Theatre in Hammersmith. Diana was delighted by the idea of the musical which she said, 'Parodied me to perfection.' However, she later admitted that the famed mink bikini was in fact made from rabbit fur. The Dennis Hamilton publicity machine was working overtime, but Diana claimed that the mink bikini idea was all hers and not Hamilton's, 'As was the popular belief by this time about everything I did.'

A Kid for Two Farthings performed well at the box office, and there was praise for Diana's performance in the film. She found that J. Lee Thompson was true to his word and gave her the lead role in *Yield to the Night*, which would be a significant step in Diana's film career.

J. Lee Thompson began his career writing plays, and then entered the film world as a scriptwriter. In 1938, he worked with Alfred Hitchcock as a dialogue coach on *Jamaica Inn*. He was fascinated by the intricate detail which permeated Hitchcock's creative process, and this would become an element of his own work as a director later on. After serving in the RAF as a tail gunner and wireless operator during the Second World War, he returned to scriptwriting, working at Elstree Studios.

His earlier work as a director included the 1950 film *Murder Without Crime*, which deals with the subject of a man convinced he has committed murder. He also made *The Yellow Balloon* (1953), which examines the story of a child blackmailed into criminality. The aforementioned *The Weak and the Wicked* (1954), based on the memoirs of Joan Henry about her life behind bars, was his biggest box office hit by that point. *Yield to the Night* perhaps signifies a continuation of that need to seek justice and give a voice to those without, asking audiences to understand the person behind the crime before judging their behaviour.

Yield to the Night (1956) tells the fictional story of Mary Hilton, a young woman facing the death penalty for murder after she shoots another woman in a crime of passion. We witness her recalling the events leading up to her imprisonment as she awaits her fate. Hilton endures the strict mundanity of her isolated confinement, closely guarded by six female wardens on rotation. She hopes for a reprieve, with each day holding the possibility of good news. Never left alone, but constantly isolated with her thoughts, we see Hilton slowly unravel under the pressure.

It is a tense and claustrophobic film, seen by many as a rallying cry for the removal of the death penalty. It is also viewed as a telling of Ruth Ellis's story, the last woman in the UK to be put to death by hanging in 1955, although this was denied by Thompson and writer Joan Henry. Henry based the screenplay on her own book and stated that this was a purely fictional account, although it shared many elements of Ellis's story. There would be a later film made of the Ruth Ellis case, Mike Newell's critically acclaimed 1985 film, *Dance with a Stranger*, starring Miranda Richardson. The screenplay for *Dance with a Stranger* was written by playwright Shelagh Delaney, who also wrote the successful 1960s play, *A Taste of Honey*.

The casting of Diana Dors in the lead role in *Yield to the Night* was inspired, and she took the opportunity to demonstrate her acting ability, winning critical praise for her performance. Diana was almost unrecognisable, swapping her usual polished, sexy look for plain prison clothes and unwashed hair. As writer Melanie Williams later reflected, the role 'confounded rather than consolidated' her image as a sex symbol. She brought an intelligent and nuanced realism to Hilton, through a thoughtful portrayal of a sensual but complicated young woman, so driven by her love for a man that she would take such drastic action.

Hilton is not a wholly sympathetic character. Unusually for a film of the period, she never repents for her crime and is often cold towards those who show her sympathy and love. Diana brings an understated complexity to the role, reflecting the agony of her situation with seemingly no reprieve, which means the audience is not without sympathy for her despite her callous actions. Her eyes directly connect with the viewer as we discover her fate, suggesting an added element of our complicity in the outcome. Casting Diana Dors also meant the film came to the attention of a wider audience, which helped to build the discussion around the topic of capital punishment. The film would go on to gain cult status with audiences, permeating popular culture and informing critical film discourse up until the present day, with the image of Diana as Mary Hilton marking a shift in British film history and creating a lasting legacy for her status as a British cultural icon.

Yield to the Night wears its political stance proudly and with passion – it is full of heart and has a strong message. It is resolutely anti-capital punishment, and through telling Hilton's story with such sympathy, the film garnered a lot of discussion around the controversial topic at a time of national debate about its future. Ironically, by the time of the film's release in 1956, a bill to abolish capital punishment had been debated in Parliament. The resulting Homicide Act of 1957 introduced a partial reform of the law on the use of the death penalty in the case of murder, and paved the way for further changes. Capital punishment was eventually suspended in the UK in 1969.

As a result of *Yield to the Night*'s success, director J. Lee Thompson would go on to build a strong reputation for socially and artistically ground-breaking films, such as the fascinating and daring portrayal of the breakdown of a marriage in *Woman in a Dressing Gown* (1957) which starred Yvonne Mitchell, Anthony Quayle and Sylvia Syms. He would also go on to find great success with the award-winning *Ice Cold in Alex* (1958) starring Sir John Mills, Sylvia Syms, Anthony Quayle and Harry Andrews. He followed this with a Hollywood career that produced popular work such as *The Guns of Navarone* in 1961 and *Cape Fear* from 1962. An important and influential filmmaker, Thompson's career mixed commercial success with smaller compelling stories of conscience and of ordinary people, and he left a lasting legacy with his varied work.

Thompson also had a big influence on Diana's film career. In addition to *Yield to the Night*, she worked with him on three other films in the 1950s, and making such a positive connection with him and writer Joan Henry led to her breakthrough role as Mary Hilton in one of the most iconic films of the decade.

Regarded as her most accomplished film performance, *Yield to the Night* should have been a turning point in Diana's career. As she later recalled, 'To this day I do not know how I got the part but thank God I did for, if nothing else, I can always say "This I did and here it is for you to see".' Yet it did not immediately lead on to the continuing success it merited. At the time, it must have felt like the beginning of an exciting chapter for her. Diana was presented to the Queen when *Yield to the Night* was screened at the Royal Command Film Performance and was apparently asked questions about the film by Her Majesty, particularly the scenes filmed inside the cell. This was something her proud and supportive mother would have loved to have seen. Diana's special moment was perhaps tinged with sadness by her absence.

She was also named the Variety Club Showbusiness Personality of the Year in early 1956, with one particular film journalist covering the event apparently referring to Hamilton as a 'Suede-shod Svengali' after observing the two of them together. According to Diana's own account, at a party at their house a few evenings later, Hamilton was still reeling from the less-than-generous nickname he had acquired. He ranted and raged, and Diana went to bed early. There was a knock at the door, and two newspaper reporters stood on the step outside, wanting to interview her. Instead of sending them away, Hamilton shouted up to Diana, demanding that she come downstairs at once. An infuriated Diana refused. It was past midnight and she was in no mood to speak to anyone, let alone the press. But an enraged Hamilton stormed upstairs demanding that she do as he said, grabbing her by the arm and dragging her towards the stairs. They struggled and, according to Diana, he pushed her and she tumbled down the stairs, landing motionless at the bottom. Her dressing gown had fallen open, displaying her nakedness to the waiting reporters. Instead of coming to her aid, Hamilton simply remarked, 'Now fucking interview her.' Diana might have been a star at last, but Hamilton always knew how to bring her crashing back down to earth.

Chapter 6

Hollywood Calling?

Despite her concerns over his behaviour, Diana did not leave Hamilton. She would sometimes plead with him to let her go, but his response was to question what she would do without him. She later admitted that his hold over her was so strong that she felt this was probably true, that she would be lost without him, 'This was the whole crux of my life with Dennis. He was amusing and strong and had the ability to push me happily along life's way…but during all those years, he frightened me with his temper.' She felt trapped financially too, as he had control of her money. His friends were her friends, now that he had managed to stifle her contact with her own. She convinced herself that each big fight would be the last, that he would apologise, and everything would change. She was also convinced that he loved her deeply, despite his unreasonable behaviour, physical abuse and extramarital affairs.

They continued their marriage, moving in 1956 to a large property on the river at Maidenhead. The extensive house, 'Woodhurst', stood in several acres of grounds and had stables, tennis courts and a swimming pool like Diana had dreamed of as a young girl. They set about building their dream home together.

Yield to the Night was chosen as the only British film at the Cannes Film Festival that year. Diana was delighted and referred to the experience as the most glittering and successful week of her life. She enjoyed the luxurious trappings of film stardom, was courted by the press and competed along with Doris Day and Susan Hayward for the Best Acting prize, which in 1956 was presented as one award for acting, with no division by gender, as it had been in 1955. Day was nominated for Alfred Hitchcock's *The Man Who Knew Too Much* (1956). The prize eventually went to Hayward for her performance in Daniel Mann's *I'll Cry Tomorrow* (1955). Diana delightedly received a standing ovation when *Yield to the Night* was screened to a rapturous reception at the festival. It was a moment in her life that remained special for her. She recalled, 'I remember looking down from the balcony of my hotel suite that evening, seeing all the lights twinkling along the Croisette, among them my own name, and hearing the roar of the crowd below. "This is my night," I thought… "Whatever happens to me in the future, no one can ever take it away".' Diana was now a film star.

She felt that she was now seen as an actress, a star in her own right, with no need for gimmicks to keep her name alive. But Hamilton did not seem keen to stop with his tricks. He decided they should buy a castle in Wales, or bid for Fort Belvedere in Surrey, the former home of Edward, Prince of Wales, which was not even on the market. He also spent her money like it was going out of fashion, on sumptuous luxuries. Diana felt his erratic energy and extravagance was unstoppable at times, and it worried her. It concerned friends and relatives too, including her father.

Diana's father, however, was also set to announce that he was moving on with his life. He told her that he was intending to marry her Aunty Kit, her mother's sister. It was barely a year since her mother had died, and this was a great shock for Diana. She refused to go to the wedding.

Diana arrived for the London premiere of *Yield to the Night* in her powder-blue Cadillac, looking fabulous in her sparkling, sequined evening gown and in her element as screaming fans lined the streets to the Haymarket Theatre.

Diana and Hamilton held an after-party at their fancy new house in Maidenhead. Entertaining was a big part of their lives. Diana reflected that Hamilton was never happier than when surrounded by people and pouring them drinks. He liked to entertain at home, so he could be the one in control, particularly of the guest list. On a rare outing to a showbiz party hosted by someone else, Bob Monkhouse was there with his wife Elizabeth and Hamilton apparently flew into a rage at the sight of him, pushing him straight out of the door: another sign, perhaps, of Hamilton's burgeoning paranoia.

Despite the critical success of *Yield to the Night*, Diana had not worked for several months. She commented that eight months passed without work after she finished the film, during which time she 'Lived gloriously without my doing anything in the way of work except to collect the Rank pay cheque.' She was still all over the tabloids, of course, thanks to Hamilton, but there was still no hint of the film star offers that Diana so desperately craved. But then Hollywood finally called.

RKO Pictures wanted a British female star to appear with comedian George Gobel in a film called *I Married a Woman*, directed by Hal Kanter and produced by Gobel's own production company. He was a big star in America at the time, but they needed a vehicle which could drive forward his success across the pond. As Diana commented, 'I had never even seen him, let alone met him, but I did know that he was one of America's top television names and that was good enough for me.'

In the film, Gobel plays hapless advertising executive Mickey Briggs, who is given 48 hours by his boss to come up with a campaign for a big client, Luxemberg Beer, and save the company from ruin. He involves his neglected wife, Janice, a former 'Miss Luxemberg' model, in the crazy campaign he comes up with to save the day. The script, developed from an original story by New York radio writer Goodman Ace, had been around for a while, with Cary Grant and Betty Drake apparently lined up for the project back in 1950. But that version never made it into production. It was to be a light and frothy affair, and RKO thought Diana would be the perfect actress to star as Janice alongside Gobel in the project. They also offered her $85,000 to do so. Diana and Hamilton would have been on the first plane out to Hollywood. Except they decided to sail on the Queen Elizabeth liner to New York first, due to Hamilton's fear of flying.

Again, *I Married a Woman* was a film that relied on Diana's looks and voluptuous figure, and the part had the usual requirements for her to be the flirty female distraction, with the film trailer concentrating on her womanly features and the tag-line 'She is! She is! She is!' It is a rather predictable light comedy of misunderstandings and the female roles are flimsy, but the dialogue has its witty moments and Gobel himself described Diana as a fine performer.

Diana was finally about to fulfil her dream of making movies in Hollywood, but she was wistful about leaving her home and apprehensive about what would await her over there. After the five-day journey, her fears subsided when she saw the Manhattan skyline and the waiting photographers, desperate to get a shot of 'Britain's Marilyn Monroe' as she arrived on their shores. RKO made sure that she had every luxury she could wish for: a limousine, tickets to the best shows in town, and PR men to sort out anything she needed. But the press kept mentioning Marilyn, which annoyed Diana greatly. They were greeted once again by the press on arrival in Los Angeles, and the head of RKO was even there to welcome them, ahead of a large press reception. A few days later, the head of production at RKO, William Dozier, offered Diana a three-picture contract supposedly worth half a million dollars. Diana didn't think twice and signed immediately. Their stay in Hollywood was to be a little longer than she and Hamilton first anticipated.

The couple rented a small house and Diana started preparations for filming at Columbia Studios. Friends flew out to join them and Hamilton tried to keep himself busy. Firstly, he insisted they buy a house in Beverly Hills. Hamilton was to discover that his hold over his wife's business dealings in the US would pan out differently than in the UK. Despite the first few weeks of exhilaration, Diana started to feel a little homesick. Although she was able to finally enjoy the luxury of swimming in her own Hollywood pool (albeit a rented one), she did not feel comfortable. Instead, she felt apprehensive and unsettled. As she reflected in her second autobiography, the dreams she had chased for so long were not what she had perhaps hoped for, 'One evening I sat alone in the pool-house among the orchids and the orange trees, gazing up at the big, floodlit white mansion…What happens now? I thought, with almost a touch of panic. This is all I ever wanted…but where do I go from here?'

Diana's friend, the celebrity hairdresser Raymond, had decided to fly out with his wife Jennifer to stay with the couple. He had an idea for a business gimmick, which would generate a bit of publicity. He would create a hairstyle especially for Diana in Hollywood. A big party was thrown to welcome him to LA, and all the great and the good whom they had met so far were invited along to enjoy their hospitality. The champagne was flowing, columnists and photographers were on hand and the stars mingled. But the relaxed atmosphere changed in the blink of an eye.

As Diana and Hamilton stood by the swimming pool chatting with her agent, Louis Schurr and Hollywood costume designer, Howard Shoup, an agency photographer jostled a couple of people who were standing near them. As a result, all four went crashing into the water. Afterwards, Hamilton pulled himself out of the pool and in his fury, he grabbed the photographer and beat him into unconsciousness. The assembled guests were horrified, the press went into a frenzy, and Diana found herself in a nightmare. The police were called and the party came to an abrupt halt. So did Diana's dreams, as the next day the newspapers were full of it, blaming Diana and Hamilton for the drunken episode, and suggesting it was a cheap stunt. Diana was horrified that anyone would think they'd set it up themselves, and she felt utterly humiliated by it at the time. She later added, 'I am somewhat of a sentimentalist and anyone who knows me at all would ridicule the idea that I would have gone in wearing Dennis's anniversary diamond watch.' It was Hamilton's reaction that had riled the press more than the original incident. One headline reportedly read, 'Go home Diana, and take Mr Dors with you!' Diana was mortified because her dream Hollywood start had come to an abrupt end.

The bosses at RKO were furious, concerned that their investment was about to potentially turn out to be a very bad one. They demanded that Diana phone all the columnists and explain, apologise and agree that her husband had acted inappropriately. She did what she was told as she was still under contract.

Diana was due to start work on her second film for RKO, *The Unholy Wife* (1957), a film noir drama set in the wine country of northern California. She was to star as a femme fatale named Phyllis, who tells her sordid story from her prison cell in flashback. Phyllis meets and marries a rich Napa Valley vintner but has a passionate affair with a local rodeo rider. She plots to kill her husband, but the plan backfires and she accidentally kills his friend instead. She confesses to her husband and tries to get him to confess to the crime, but eventually fate intervenes when her mother-in-law is poisoned and Phyllis is blamed. She is sent to prison for a crime she did not commit and faces the death penalty, the punishment she seemingly deserves. Shelley Winters had originally been considered for the role, but as Diana was now under contract to RKO, it was she who took the lead.

Diana and Hamilton flew out to the Napa Valley but she was apprehensive about the shoot. The director, John Farrow, had a fearsome reputation, but she actually found she worked well with him. Her co-star on the film was Rod Steiger, star of dramatic films such as *On the Waterfront* (1954) and *The Harder They Fall* (1956). Diana was very impressed with Steiger and his acting skills. She also fell deeply and passionately in love with him.

Desperate for love and affection, and to break free from Hamilton's constant grasp, Diana was perhaps vulnerable to meeting someone else at that point. She had endured five years of Hamilton and his unreasonable behaviour, and his actions had almost sent her Hollywood dreams unravelling. She was tired of it all. Still only 24, she craved affection to fill the void left by her troubled marriage. Diana reflected that Steiger made her feel like a woman for once, not like a child to be hidden away and cosseted. Working with him on set inspired her and made her want to be a better actor too. She was free to be able to think about the art, rather than how to play for publicity for once.

But her feelings for Steiger were overwhelming. She tried to keep them to herself but one evening she broke down and confessed all to Hamilton. Inevitably, his reaction was one of anger and the next day, he apparently entered the RKO lot brandishing a shotgun, demanding to see Steiger. He was out of luck on that front as Steiger was keeping a low profile now that the news was out.

Diana was summoned into the office of producer Bill Dozier, who demanded that she end things with 'lover boy'. They were both married and the storm of negative publicity that would be created by an affair between them would cause untold headaches for the studio. There was also the 'morals clause' in her contract to consider, under which she could be sent out on her ear. Diana started to realise how much of her was now owned by the studio. Despite her protestations of being madly in love with Steiger, she knew she had to listen. In her mind it was more than just a passing fling, but she did what she was told.

Hamilton decided to fly back to the UK, but rather than try to stop him as he perhaps hoped, Diana helped him pack. She would be free from him at last! She continued to see Steiger, but they were not as careful as they should have been because word spread of their affair and the press went to town. Dozier summoned Hamilton back to LA, insisting that he and Diana play the happy couple for the cameras. But Diana yearned for

Steiger and still felt hopelessly in love with him. It was unbearable for her to be parted from him, and to be unable to speak to him in front of anyone on set. They crept around, seeing each other under the cloak of darkness when they could, and spending time at his beachfront home in Malibu.

Hamilton grew impatient and flew back to the UK yet again. According to Diana, he set about breaking up other people's marriages in the same way his had been, and went on a rampage of sex. Amongst the alleged conquests were the wives of friends, and apparently the then young, up-and-coming star, Shirley Anne Field, according to Diana's account.

As filming drew to a close on *The Unholy Wife*, Diana knew she would have to say goodbye to Steiger. He flew to New York to sort things out with his wife and from there, she received the inevitable call from him to say that it was over between him and Diana. She was distraught and could not imagine life without him.

When *The Unholy Wife* was finally released, it was badly received by critics. The *New York Times* was particularly scathing, describing the film as 'Pretentiously tinted in garish color, and staged with coronation pomp by director-producer John Farrow, the picture is a hollow, tawdry little drama of frustration, violence and a loveless marriage,' and suggesting Diana should stick to comedy roles.

Diana hung around in Hollywood for a while, dating various handsome would-be stars, but there were no new films on the horizon, no exciting social engagements to keep her occupied, and no press interest. She returned home to the UK on a grey November day, alone, and describing herself as 'a fallen idol'.

She could not return home to the house she shared with Hamilton in Maidenhead; instead, she took a suite at the Dorchester Hotel in London's Park Lane. Despite her earnings from the films she made for RKO, her money had gone, apparently due to Hamilton's business failings. Hamilton tried to win her back and she returned to their home to talk, with the press camped outside for days waiting for them to emerge. They eventually appeared for the waiting cameras, announcing a reconciliation. But Diana was not happy about it and was just resigned to the inevitability of it through lack of willpower. She recalled, 'The bird was back in its cage; its flight for freedom had failed.'

Diana and Hamilton continued with the charade of their marriage. They entertained friends at Christmas 1956, and the house was full of merriment and laughter. But Hamilton was still sleeping with other women and Diana was just as unhappy in her gilded cage. He was still controlling her business dealings, with Diana apparently knowing little about what this meant for her career long-term. Through an old friend, she discovered that Rod Steiger had also been involved with another young actress she knew. That bubble had burst for her too.

Resigned to her fate and seemingly back to square one again in her acting career, Diana reverted to type and started filming with Victor Mature on *The Long Haul* (1957), a British drama directed by Ken Hughes about an American ex-serviceman who moves to Liverpool at the behest of his English wife and finds work as a lorry driver, only to become mixed up with a group of criminals. Filmed at Shepperton Studios and essentially a procedural B-film, it was originally to star Robert Mitchum before Mature signed up. Diana plays the highly sexualised female lead, Lynn, a woman with a past and an intensity in every glance or gesture. Considering the limited scope of the character and the script, she brings all that she can to her performance. She looks stunning, with screen presence worthy of a Hollywood noir, but sadly this jars considerably with the very British location and feel of the film. Her glamour seems incongruous in a Glasgow greasy spoon truck stop. But Diana and an equally out-of-sorts Mature have screen chemistry, even though she perhaps outplays him in every scene.

Diana recalled having a great time filming with Mature, who often proclaimed himself to be the world's worst actor, and that he was quite a character, 'I adore Vic as a person but he is hell to work with…he clowns all the time, especially when drama is called for.'

Hamilton was worried about Mature because he had a reputation with the ladies that perhaps rivalled his own. Diana and Mature got on well during filming, but she was not attracted to him. She was, however, attracted to his on-set double. Diana and the young, handsome and sweet-natured Tommy Yeardye started to spend a lot of time together on set. Diana was lonely, Yeardye was the right sort of man to fulfil her needs and the timing was right. They began an on-set fling. Unlike some of the

A blue plaque at The Haven Nursing Home in Swindon marks Diana's birthplace in 1931. (*Author's image*)

Diana's family home in Marlborough Road, Swindon. (*Author's image*)

An infant Diana poses for the camera
(date unknown). (*Alamy*)

An early portrait of Diana as a young
actress, late 1940s. (*Alamy*)

Diana with Kenneth Griffith in *The Shop at Sly Corner* (1946), her first film role. (*Alamy*)

As Charlotte in *Oliver Twist* (1948). (*Alamy*)

With Flora Robson in *Good-Time Girl* (1948). (*Alamy*)

Appearing with John McCallum in *A Boy, A Girl and a Bike* (1949). (*Alamy*)

Diana's first lead role as Dora Bracken in *Diamond City* (1949). (*Alamy*)

'The female Errol Flynn'. Diana meets controversial actor Errol Flynn at a garden party organised by *The Sunday Pictorial Newspaper* in June 1952. (*MirrorPix*)

Diana with her first husband, Dennis
Hamilton, in 1953. The couple
married in 1951 when Diana was 19.
(*MirrorPix*)

The face of 1950s British cinema. Diana
in a publicity photo from 1953. (*Alamy*)

Diana with Joe Robinson in a publicity shot for *A Kid for Two Farthings* (1955). (*Alamy*)

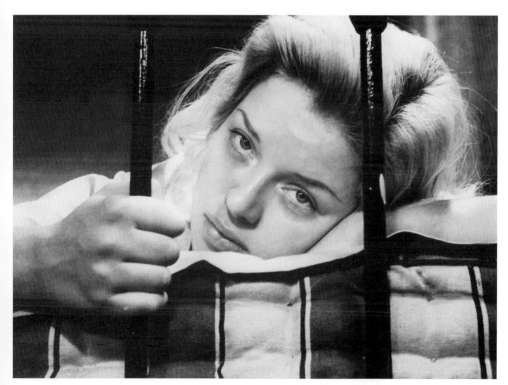

Diana's most famous role, as Mary Hilton, in *Yield to the Night* (1956). (*Alamy*)

Diana surrounded by autograph hunters at the Cannes Film Festival in May 1956. (*MirrorPix*)

A publicity shot for *The Unholy Wife* (1957). (*Alamy*)

A still from British noir *Tread Softly Stranger* (1958). (*Alamy*)

With second husband Dickie Dawson in 1959, the year they married. (*Alamy*)

Diana in Madrid in 1961. (*Alamy*)

Diana with her sons Mark and Gary in 1966. (*Alamy*)

With Joan Crawford, Judy Geeson and Ty Hardin on the set of *Berserk!* (1967). (*Alamy*)

Diana marries third husband Alan Lake on 11 November 1968. (*Alamy*)

Diana in 1968. (*Alamy*)

Diana walks through Leeds
Market as she films scenes for
Queenie's Castle in 1970. (*Alamy*)

Diana at home with her youngest son, Jason (date unknown). (*Alamy*)

Diana with Harry H. Corbett in the 1973 film, *Steptoe and Son Ride Again*. (*MirrorPix*)

Diana appears in *Hammer House of Horror – The Children of the Full Moon* in 1980. (*Alamy*)

Diana with Alan Lake and their son Jason in January 1982. (*MirrorPix*)

Alan Lake and son Jason at Diana's funeral on 11 May 1984. (*Alamy*)

A statue of Diana in Swindon, her home town. (*Author's image*)

Diana in April 1984.
(*MirrorPix*)

A lasting screen icon - Diana in a
publicity photo from 1958. (*Alamy*)

young men she encountered, Yeardye had no delusions of grandeur and was happy to just be a stand-in, doing stunts and riding horses for the leading men. She later recalled, 'I had had enough of being dominated and manoeuvred. At 25 years of age I seemed to have been married all my life, yet never lived, so it was only natural that I wanted a little fun.' Diana assumed it would be a short fling that would end when the filming did. But she was wrong.

Relations with Hamilton were still strained and she did not trust him at all. She worried that he was still cheating on her, but his behaviour was increasingly erratic at home. In her 1981 autobiography, Diana recalls an incident when the couple were having dinner at home with comedian and actor Jon Pertwee and his then wife, fellow performer Jean Marsh. The women were chatting in private, talking about men and Diana mentioned her attraction to Yeardye. What she did not know was that Hamilton had been secretly recording the conversation, something he often did when guests were present as a prank to entertain himself. Hysterical with anger, he confronted the two of them about their conversation, breaking furniture and ornaments in his rage. He then ordered the two women to leave the house. After a few days, Diana had to return to him. She had a film to complete and money to earn, so she flew back into her cage.

Diana was one of the first celebrities to appear on popular television show *This Is Your Life*, with Eamonn Andrews surprising her at a night out at the theatre in early 1957. Invited guests included her father and her Aunty Kit, and her elocution teacher from her teens, and Diana cried unashamedly. There was another surprise for both her and Hamilton when the photographer who had pushed them into the swimming pool in Hollywood walked out as a guest. Hamilton resisted the urge to punch him this time, instead enduring a reluctant handshake.

Whilst Diana continued filming for *The Long Haul*, she was still going home to a difficult atmosphere with Hamilton and his unpredictable behaviour every night. One evening, completely without warning, Hamilton announced that he had met someone else and was leaving her. The next morning as she left for filming, she recalls a subdued Hamilton saying he would not be there when she returned home that night. She lingered a moment, caught up in the mix of nostalgia for the good times they had shared and perhaps habit, but then left. She did not try to talk him out of it or ask him to stay. When she returned that evening, he had gone.

Delighted to finally be free, Diana organised a party to celebrate the next evening and invited Yeardye and some of his friends. The next morning, the spring weather was glorious, so Diana, Yeardye and another couple went for a drive out into the country. When they returned to Diana's home, however, they were met in the drive by her housekeeper, who told them that Hamilton was in the house waiting for her. He apparently wanted her to sign some papers. As he had been dealing with her business affairs for so long, Diana was used to being asked to 'sign papers', so rather than make a scene with Hamilton, she asked Yeardye and their friends to wait in the car.

According to her autobiography, she entered the house and climbed the stairs, only to find Hamilton stood at the top brandishing a shotgun. Shaking, she walked towards him, unsure what to do for the best. He asked her to sign a piece of paper, which he claimed was a list of all the men she had been unfaithful with during their marriage. He then produced another document, signing over all her assets to him, including the house, the coffee bar, the cars, all her cash and even her beloved boxer dog. Given the situation, signing the documents and getting out of the house seemed like the safest thing to do. Yet before she could leave, he started smashing things, including a window through which he threatened to shoot Yeardye who was still outside. Hamilton apparently punched Diana in the head and she fell to the floor. Dazed and confused, she knew that Yeardye had arrived and was struggling with Hamilton. She was taken to Yeardye's parents' house and was seen by a doctor, who said that the blow from Hamilton had punctured her eardrum. Despite choosing not to press charges against him, Diana knew that this was the final nail in the coffin of her marriage.

Other accounts of the evening, including from Hamilton and Yeardye, apparently refute this version of events, suggesting there was no gun involved and no broken windows. The idea of Diana signing her assets over to Hamilton in this manner has also been downplayed over the years, with some writers suggesting that this was a convenient excuse to tell the taxman.

Either way, when she returned to Woodhurst to pick up some clothes and possessions, they were piled up in the driveway waiting for her and she needed to find somewhere else to live. After finally finishing filming on *The Long Haul*, papers were drawn up, solicitors were involved and property was dished out. Diana stayed in the penthouse they had shared and Hamilton moved into another property in the Woodhurst grounds, practically next door with just a garden fence dividing them.

Diana flew out to Italy to film *La Ragazza Del Palio* (1958), a French-Italian production in which she starred as an American quiz show winner called Diana Dixon who spends her money on a trip to Italy. When her new Cadillac breaks down near Siena in Tuscany, she meets Prince Piero di Montalcino (Vittorio Gassman), a handsome Italian nobleman. Dixon assumes he must be wealthy and he thinks the same of her. But appearances can be deceptive. The film was directed by Luigi Zampa, who had a long career in Italian cinema, and it was known as *The Love Specialist* in America. It culminates in scenes at the Palio horse race, reflected in the film's title.

Yeardye also flew out to Rome to be with her, as did his parents for a short holiday. Diana felt that her time out there with Yeardye was rather romantic. He was a calm and steady influence, particularly after her whirlwind time with Hamilton. She recalled, 'Tommy to me, apart from being attractive, was like a strong oak tree against which I could lean and catch my breath after the tumultuous years of living with Dennis.' But Diana was starting to lose interest in him a little, perhaps missing the spark she had felt with other, less predictable men.

Back in the UK, living next door to her estranged husband became a rather surreal experience for Diana, especially witnessing what she referred to as his 'playboy existence'. He occasionally made contact, apparently with attempts to win her back, but according to Diana, her life with Yeardye was steady and uncomplicated. But she also missed her Svengali and felt tired of 'controlling her own destiny' at times. After all, Hamilton had controlled so much of her life. She was tempted.

Diana was also tempted by the return of Rod Steiger. According to her autobiography, they met again in New York when she was filming an appearance on the *Perry Como Show*, and 'rekindled some spark of fire'. According to Diana, their brief reconciliation was quite a stormy affair.

She also felt conflicted over Yeardye and Hamilton. But back in England, Diana and Yeardye continued as normal.

Diana recalls that on an evening out at a cabaret show, she was introduced to one of the acts, the comedian Dickie Dawson. She liked his wit and swagger, and invited him to visit her sometime. He immediately suggested the following Sunday. Diana hastily arranged a party, inviting her old friend Michael Caborn-Waterfield and his brother John amongst others. Throughout the evening, however, they kept hearing strange noises emanating from Hamilton's flat next door. The guests found it rather amusing but Diana was concerned. One of the guests at the party, who Diana referred to only as 'the stuntman', was not exactly a fan of Dennis Hamilton, having been in a dispute with him over a girl. He kept making insinuations about taking his revenge on him. Diana thought little of it as he would not be the first man to want to make Hamilton pay for a misdemeanour.

A short time later, someone finally did take revenge on Hamilton. Diana was having a party with friends on Boxing Day night while Hamilton was away from home. In the early hours, as the guests started to thin out, there was suddenly a large explosion outside. They rushed to the window to see Hamilton's prized boat, which was moored nearby, engulfed in flames. The police soon arrived, as did the press. Hamilton arrived home devastated. Diana recounts the incident in her autobiography, and suggests that Hamilton immediately suspected her and her friends, prompting a series of reprisal attacks on her property by his associates. She felt that it was too dangerous for her to stay and sold her property at Woodhurst. In the spring of 1958, she bought a farmhouse in the Sussex countryside for her and Yeardye to live in: a quiet and reflective space away from the memories at Maidenhead.

Just before the move to Sussex, Diana had made *Tread Softly Stranger* (1958), a British crime drama directed by Gordon Parry and starring George Baker and Terence Morgan alongside Diana. It is a gritty black and white noir-style drama, set in the fictional industrial town of Rawborough in northern England. It was adapted from the stage play, *Blind Alley* (1953) by Jack Popplewell and location shots were filmed in Rotherham. In the film, Johnny Mansell (George Baker) has fled to his hometown after racking up large gambling debts in London. He is forced to move into a cramped flat with his brother Dave (Terence Morgan), who works as a clerk in the local steel mill, and Dave's girlfriend Calico, played by Diana, a hostess in a local nightclub. With money so tight, Calico comes up with a plan to pay off their debts, asking the brothers to steal the payroll money from the steel mill.

On the surface, *Tread Softly Stranger* appeared to be a typical British noir film, but it had a grittiness and authenticity that stood it apart, particularly when film critics revisited it in later years. The cinematography by Douglas Slocombe was given particular credence for its use of locations and the feeling of everyday life it brought to the screen. Slocombe made his name with the Ealing Studios output of the 1940s and 1950s, and went on to work with Steven Spielberg on the first three *Indiana Jones* films. He was nominated three times for an Academy Award for his work.

Diana gives a nuanced performance as the somewhat improbably named Calico, whose clever plotting makes for entertaining viewing as she plays the brothers off against each other. From her very first scene, it is obvious what sort of girl she is supposed to be. Hers is a kind of northern bedsit glamour, at odds with the gritty surroundings of a town like Rawborough, but you can see why any man might be swayed by her insistence to do the wrong thing. The frustration at being stuck in a small town is palpable in her performance: we never really understand her inner motivation, but we sense there is a deeper story there. In many ways, the role in *Tread Softly Stranger* feels like it epitomises Diana's own film career at that stage of the 1950s.

Diana did not miss the parties, noise and action from Woodhurst, and she welcomed the peace and quiet of her new home. But she was tiring of Yeardye. She felt he never really did anything, either for her or himself, and she was finding life with him dull. As she recalled later, 'When you finally fall out of bed, you've got to have something to talk about,' as a Hollywood producer had once advised her. She had come to realise that she and Yeardye did not. She was also concerned again for her film career. *The Long Haul* had not performed well at the box office. There were no calls from Hollywood after she had burned her bridges there with the swimming pool incident and negative press coverage. Indeed, the only notoriety she had was the press interest in her tumultuous personal life. She felt this was putting producers off from considering her for potential roles.

When she was offered a role in *Passport to Shame* (1958), she practically bit off the hands of the producers. The film, directed by first-time filmmaker Alvin Rakoff, deals with the subject of organised prostitution rackets on the streets of 1950s Soho. A taxi driver called Johnny, played by Eddie Constantine, is conned into marrying a French girl called Mallou (Odile Versois) to give her a British passport, so she can be forced into prostitution by crime boss, Nick (Herbert Lom). Diana plays prostitute Vicki, who is trying to raise enough money to pay hospital bills for her sister Maria, who has been scarred for life in an acid attack by the vicious Nick. Diana gives Vicki a world-weary edge, suggesting a young woman who is tired of the life she is living but is too jaded to find a way out. She has seen it all before and does not easily trust anyone. Her cynicism is an interesting contrast with Mallou's innocence. There are, perhaps, parallels with Diana's own life at play here too; although a young woman still in her twenties, she had experienced life's challenges at pace.

Passport to Shame is a gritty and uncomfortable film, which explores the seedy underworld being played out on London's streets. The atmospheric soundtrack also adds to the sleazy feel. Diana's role requires her to stand around in figure-hugging outfits and fancy underwear rather a lot, and the film has been criticised for its 'sexploitation' undertones, which on the surface is an interesting clash with its supposed condemnation of the Soho sex trade and the exploitation of the women caught up in it. The film is also notable for its incredibly small budget, which Rakoff himself apparently referred to as 'no budget rather than low budget'. There are uncredited early career appearances by Michael Caine and Jackie Collins. Joan Sims also appears, giving a delightful performance as a phone operator in the taxi office. Nicholas Roeg, the acclaimed director of *Don't Look Now* (1973) and *The Man Who Fell to Earth* (1976), worked as a camera operator on the film.

Due to the low budget for *Passport to Shame*, Diana's fee was smaller than she was now used to, but that was inevitable, given she was now a slightly riskier prospect with the baggage of publicity she brought to any production. Headlines such as 'Why did the bubble burst?' were typical.

In the 1958 *Picturegoer* Film Annual, an article entitled 'The Blondes Go Bust' talked about her fall from favour, referring to her and other blonde stars like Marilyn Monroe and Jane Mansfield as being all but washed up, 'They've slipped so badly that all their ballyhoo won't pull them round.' It went on to highlight that for Diana, 'Two mediocre Hollywood films and headlined rows have cost Diana Dors a lot of popularity'. She still filled column inches, but not for the right reasons.

Once filming on *Passport to Shame* finished, Diana dabbled with the idea of a business deal fronting her own brand of shampoo for Woolworth's. But eager to do something with more immediate financial benefits, she accepted the offer of another variety theatre tour. The show's agent was Joe Collins, father of Joan and Jackie Collins. There were various acts on his books to fill the Diana Dors Show with, but he needed a good comedian to warm up the audience. Diana recalls that it was Yeardye who suggested Dickie Dawson for the spot.

Diana very much enjoyed the prospect of working with Dawson. She found him to be great company, and she loved his wit and his looks. She was looking forward to the tour. She left Yeardye back in London and set off with her small entourage for the first stop in Coventry. Again, Diana's apparent lack of money management skills came into play, as she recalled leaving £11,000 in cash in a safety deposit box back in London, entrusting Yeardye with the key should he need anything. This turned out, according to Diana, not to be the best idea she had ever had.

After spending so much time together on what turned out to be a successful variety tour, Diana realised that she had fallen in love with Dawson. They had a connection that she felt she simply did not have with Yeardye. When she told Yeardye, he did not take it well. She wrote in her autobiography that he took all of the £11,000 from her safety deposit box in London and disappeared. Despite the fact that the existence of the money had not been revealed to the taxman, after trying to locate Yeardye and find out what had happened, Diana felt she had no choice but to go to the police and report the missing money. Inevitably, it was splashed all over the newspapers. Diana decided not to press charges against Yeardye, and the matter was resolved in private. He apparently accused her of stealing eighteen months of his life. In her 1979 book *Behind Closed Doors*,

Diana later referred to their relationship as 'my muscleman era. I suppose everyone goes through a strange time in their lives when they fancy certain individuals – only to look back and wonder what the attraction was'. The end of one love affair meant she was free to start another one with Dawson.

Chapter 7

Family and Fame

Like many of the men that Diana fell for, Dickie Dawson was somewhat of an enigma. The life and soul of the party, quick-witted and cheeky, he was an entertainer who could make her laugh. She felt he was always filled with ideas and a perfect match for her personality. But he was also fiercely ambitious and determined to become a big star. Dawson's real name was Colin Emm, and he seemingly came from simple working-class roots. But Diana was never quite comfortable with the life story he told her and could never quite grasp at the truth, which seemed to float away like gossamer when she tried. But his vibrancy brought a new spark into Diana's life and she was happy. They lived together on the farm in Sussex quite happily. Diana inevitably had to employ staff to actually manage the farm itself, for what she and Dawson knew about managing it could be written on a postage stamp.

Her troubled contract with RKO was eventually terminated by the studio after it invoked the 'morals clause' that had been threatened previously when she had been involved with the married actor Rod Steiger. This time, it was in response to tabloid articles accusing her of cavorting topless at a party, which she denied. Her cancelled contract left her out of pocket, but she did eventually settle the dispute with them in 1961. She successfully sued *The New York Enquirer* too, which had run the story. Her money issues did not end there: she was in trouble for not declaring all of the money she earned for *Tread Softly Stranger* and she needed cash. She terminated her Rank contract and accepted a much smaller settlement sum. Rank, having no films in the pipeline for her anyway, must have thought Christmas had come early.

Shortly after Diana left them, the Rank Organisation quietly began letting contracts expire, and by 1961, the company was on its knees financially. A few high-profile flops and a change in society's entertainment habits meant it no longer had the sway it once held in the industry. Its film productions were wound down and its cinemas were sold off to become casinos and bingo halls. The extensive back catalogue of films was sold. Ironically, these films could now be seen on television, which was now the visual medium of choice for the British public, who were choosing to stay in and watch the box instead of going to the cinema. In its heyday, J. Arthur Rank's empire had employed 34,000 people, but now it was reduced to selling off the family silver in order to survive. The films of its golden period in the mid-twentieth century are still enjoyed by many as British film classics, but the influence of Rank across all aspects of the British cinema industry has become a long-forgotten memory for most. It was ultimately the beginning of the death knell for the traditional British film studios that had dominated for so long and influenced so many.

Diana rekindled contact with Dennis Hamilton, with the occasional friendly phone call. There was always going to be a connection there, no matter what. She had heard from mutual friends that his health had not been great. She just could not imagine him being unwell or without the boundless energy that always seemed to emanate from him. Hamilton had sold Woodhurst and his Maidenhead coffee bar to the notorious landlord Perec 'Peter' Rachman to solve his own cash flow problems. Rachman became a slum landlord, with a seedy empire of tiny bedsits in west London, rented out to the poor and desperate, who were left to live in appalling conditions. But Rachman also owned various nightclubs and brothels, and was the boyfriend of Mandy Rice-Davies, who later found notoriety through her involvement in the Profumo scandal in the 1960s. As well as selling his coffee bar to Rachman, Hamilton rented out his other business, and moved back to a small but luxurious flat in London's Belgravia. He was admitted to hospital with a heart condition, insisting he was dying to anyone that would listen. But he also agreed to a divorce, allowing Diana to be free to marry Dawson, whom Hamilton actually liked.

Diana herself had started to develop health problems. She experienced terrible stomach pains and was eventually diagnosed with pancreatitis, being prescribed morphine at one stage as the pain was so severe. But Dawson stuck attentively and lovingly by her side throughout her illness.

After she recovered, there was a small flurry of work: a trip to South Africa to appear in cabaret in Johannesburg and a contract to appear on *The Steve Allen Show* in America early in 1959. Steve Allen was a very big deal across the pond. At that stage, the all-round TV and radio personality, and later co-creator of the *Tonight Show*, hosted his own television variety sketch show, which featured an array of stars each week and launched many comedy and music careers. The show gave Elvis Presley his first television appearance, amongst others. The prospect of Diana appearing with Allen particularly thrilled Dawson, who had ambitions to make it big in the US himself.

However, little cracks were starting to appear in their relationship. For the most part, they were very happy and she still loved his energy. But Dawson was showing himself to be jealous, mainly of other men. This was a small issue to begin with; there were momentary reactions from him and Diana put the thought of it out of her mind. They enjoyed Christmas 1958 together at home in Sussex, before flying out to New York for *The Steve Allen Show*. The night before they left, Dennis Hamilton rang Diana from the hospital. He once again mentioned the boat explosion, and they had a slightly sparky conversation about it before Diana told him she needed to get ready for her trip. His goodbye sounded and felt very final to Diana, as she recalled that he ended the call by saying, 'I will not be seeing you again…I will not be here when you come back.'

The trip to New York was successful and her experience on *The Steve Allen Show* was fruitful, leading to further, well-paid appearances on the programme. Diana and Dawson flew on to California for a short break. She had not been back to Hollywood since her ill-fated trip a couple of years previously, but Dawson assured her it would be OK. He was dying to be there and experience the place he had always dreamed of conquering. They visited friends and had an enjoyable time. Returning to the place in which they were staying with friends, Diana received a call from a British film writer she was familiar with, who was based in Hollywood. She did not want to speak to him, but listened in to the message being taken by her friend. Dennis Hamilton was dead.

Still reeling from the shock, Diana flew home immediately. The press was inevitably waiting for her when she arrived, firing questions at her about Hamilton and her reaction to his death. Once alone, she thought about him and their time together, 'Dennis had gone. Nothing could bring him back; that terrifying, vibrant, charming man who seemed indestructible.'

Dennis Hamilton was just 34 when he died on 3 January 1959. It was all over the newspapers, and ironically, he would probably have loved generating all that publicity. Despite his behaviour throughout their turbulent marriage, and her knowledge of his questionable dealings with other people, Diana wrote about him with great affection in her autobiography when recalling the events around his death. Although he had never discussed matters of faith before, Hamilton apparently converted to Catholicism just three days before he died. He therefore had a Catholic funeral. The flowers from Diana read: 'To my darling Dennis, with loving memories that words will never express. My love always. Diana'. She also gave him a private epitaph, a poem not for public consumption, which included the lines, 'A song of things past, of joyous things, and tears that gave it sadness. Of moments which were wonderful and good, and bitter-sweet remembrances.'

The funeral was quite a spectacle. Diana attended alone without Dawson. Many people lined the streets outside the Catholic church in Spanish Place, Marylebone, giving it the feel of a film premiere rather than a funeral. The ornate church was a fitting backdrop for the over-the-top Hamilton. Diana sat at the front of the church, but there were many women in attendance who had also known Hamilton well. As Diana later commented, 'Most were weeping into their tiny handkerchiefs, but few could conceal their curiosity about their rivals.' The funeral was quite a send-off but, of course, Dennis Hamilton had always loved a party.

Diana later discovered the cause of his death to be tertiary syphilis. Doctors suggested he had caught it many years previously, but eventually it had affected his brain, eyes and finally, his heart. The random nature of some of his behaviours and reactions now made sense to Diana. In her mind, his 'brainstorms', violent outbursts and sexual misbehaviour were probably caused by the effects of the infection, 'Now at last I knew what had been wrong with the man I married. A man who, when not bedevilled by these symptoms, could be a kind, gentle, artistic and loving person.'

Yet history has not been kind to Dennis Hamilton, and many have commented since on his behaviour, unsavoury character traits and questionable associations. They have described him as a physical bully, and have also highlighted his controlling nature towards Diana. 'Hamilton ensured that her acting was sacrificed to her 'celebrity' status,' wrote one journalist. His reputation for sexual misbehaviour and his infamous parties, with their focus on 'a hundred percent sex', are now synonymous with his overall character.

Despite his treatment of her during their marriage, Hamilton was a major part of Diana's life, so her ambiguous attitude towards him is perhaps understandable. As she commented in her 1960 autobiography, not long after his death, 'Six years as his wife have left scars on my soul that time and my present happiness cannot completely erase.' Yet she continued sporadic contact with him until his death. Even afterwards, with the hindsight of middle-age and experience, she continued to almost excuse his behaviour. The illness that was revealed after his death was, perhaps, a convenient excuse to shy away from her own inability to deal with her feelings and his unacceptable behaviour when they were together. She had been incredibly young when they married, and society at that time still pressured women into staying with a man at all costs, particularly if he had control of the purse strings like Hamilton. Ultimately, the continual 'happiness and unhappiness' complexity of her relationship with Hamilton, and the emotional hold he had over her, would come to influence the rest of her life.

As Hamilton had apparently managed Diana's business affairs as well as his own, the prospect of sorting out the financial mess that he had left behind was a daunting one. Again, Diana faced interest from lawyers and the taxman. But the contents of Hamilton's final will were quite a surprise to everyone. All he had left was £800, which he bequeathed to his parents. Where had the rest of it gone? The properties and business interests? The newspapers were fascinated that Hamilton had left nothing to Diana. She knew that she was liable for his debts and faced the prospect of bankruptcy. She placed in trust everything she owned, and buckled down for the financial fallout of Hamilton's passing.

Diana was under contract to appear on *The Steve Allen Show* in New York during this complex time. So, she fulfilled her duties, flying back and forth across the Atlantic. Dawson decided they should get married and Diana reluctantly agreed to a quick, seven-minute-long wedding in New York. They married on 12 April 1959. At the glitzy post-wedding party, attended by celebrities and the press, Diana knew hardly a soul. It was a lonely feeling. Now suddenly she was 'Mrs Dawson', and in just eight weeks, she had gone from being the estranged Mrs Hamilton, to widow and then to newly-wed.

Dawson now insisted on being called Richard instead of Dickie, and Diana felt he changed almost from the moment they said their vows, 'Gone was the man who made me laugh all the time...now I found myself living with a man who could not be spoken to until well past noon, who stopped amusing me alone unless there was an audience.'

Back home in the UK, the newly-weds set about settling into married life. Diana had followed up the opportunity for her own line of shampoo products by that stage, so her focus was on more than just acting. She commented that she was not as keen as she used to be on film acting, 'I have enough self-respect not to want to be in any more stinkers.'

The irony of her appearance in the gimmicky 'Smell-O-Vision' 1960 film *Scent of a Mystery*, where odours relating to the story were released into the cinema along with each plot twist, probably was not lost on her. The film, directed by Jack Cardiff, stars Denholm Elliot as a mystery novelist and Elizabeth Taylor as an American heiress. *Scent of a Mystery* was produced by Mike Todd, Jr., who had, with his father Mike Todd, produced such cinema spectacles as *This is Cinerama* (1952) and *Around the World in Eighty Days* (1956). Todd made wild claims to promote the film such as, 'I hope it's the kind of picture they call a scentsation!', but the huge cost of the Smell-O-Vision system and its technical problems meant it was rarely shown in conventional cinemas. The film was released in Cinerama under the title *Holiday in Spain*, but unfortunately without Smell-O-Vision. The concept did not catch on, but the film was restored and re-released in 2012, and screened in all its Smell-O-Vision glory a few years later in selected cinemas.

Diana knew she needed to use her brain as much as her body now she was older. She demonstrated a sense of perspective about her career prospects even then, understanding the limitations that her good looks would place on her: 'Now I think the worst thing in the world to be would be an ageing glamour queen…I would rather become a fat, frowsy character actress when the time comes.'

Dawson wrote the scripts for her new venture, a television variety vehicle *The Diana Dors Show*, which would eventually run for two series on ITV. The pilot was a success, with special guests, Oscar-winning singer and actress Shirley Jones and her husband, Jack Cassidy, father of future pop star, David. Diana demonstrated her variety skills with comedy sketches, singing and dancing, and performed impressions including Marlene Dietrich and, with some irony, Marilyn Monroe. But just as they were planning future shows, Diana discovered she was pregnant.

Happily for Diana, Dawson's reaction to the news could not have been more different to that of Hamilton some years before, and he was delighted at the prospect of becoming a father. And at 28, Diana felt ready to start a family. They quit the rural farm life and moved to Virginia Water in Surrey, ready to make a home for their new family. Facing the prospect of quitting work to raise a child, and with Dawson's earning potential quite low, when Diana was approached by the *News of the World* newspaper to sell her story for a very large sum, she agreed. It would run as a twelve-week serialisation starting in late January and net her £35,000, which in 1960 was a huge amount. Even after her agent's fee and a pay-out to a disgruntled writer Hamilton had previously done a deal with, Diana hoped the benefits would outweigh the bad.

Inevitably, the coverage focused on the lurid and the sensational, with much made of her private life with Hamilton, intimate secrets, and the sex parties and voyeurism. Apparently ghost-written, it became an onslaught of 'Scandal on a Sunday' week after week and increased sales for the newspaper by around 100,000. But Diana was in trouble financially, particularly when faced with Hamilton's debts and seeming mismanagement of her affairs, and it was a price worth paying for her. It was also the start of a new way of capitalising on celebrity culture and influence. Diana was one of the country's first 'celebrities' and certainly the first to 'sell her story' for a large sum, but she would not be the last personality to do so; there was a cultural shift towards the power of celebrity and the media's role in harnessing and exploiting it which has endured ever since.

Of course, such sensational coverage would have an effect on her career prospects and bring strained relationships with those close to her, including her father. And despite being prepared for a reaction, she perhaps had underestimated just how much of a stir the articles would cause. Even the Archbishop of Canterbury waded in with a reaction, denouncing her as a 'wayward hussy'. Her behaviour, and that of the British media, was debated in parliament. Decency campaigners such as Baroness Stocks were fuming, and questioned her capacity to be a good mother. This was 1960 and the country was not yet entering the progressive years of sexual and social freedom it would experience later in the decade.

In October that year, Penguin Books was brought to trial under the Obscene Publications Act, 1959, after it published the full unedited edition of D. H. Lawrence's *Lady Chatterley's Lover* in Britain. The trial was a test of the new obscenity law as the 1959 Act had made it possible for publishers to escape conviction if they could show that a work was of literary merit. The Chief Prosecutor in the trial, Mervyn Griffith-Jones, famously asked if it were the kind of book 'you would wish your wife or servants to read', and the prosecution was ridiculed for being so out of touch with changing society. Penguin Books was found not guilty and the 1961 edition of the book was dedicated to the trial jury.

It was also a few years before the 1963 Profumo affair, involving model Christine Keeler in a scandal that rocked the government and society to the core. The UK did not enjoy a 'permissive society' and generally found Diana's alleged behaviour, as described in the *News of the World* serialisation, disgusting. But many more women would appear in the nation's Sunday tabloids that decade to tell their side of the story, including Christine Keeler and Mandy Rice-Davies during the Profumo scandal.

Diana's friends and acquaintances decided to have their say too, cashing in perhaps on her infamy. Even her scorned lover, Tommy Yeardye, gave his account of his life with Diana. As she later recalled, 'For a year Tommy revelled under the title of Diana Dors' ex-boyfriend…but I knew it was only a matter of time before the excitement went stale.' She also cheekily added, 'I do not bear him any grudge, why should I? Thankfully he has made a success of his life, for there was not much future in "falling off horses in films" as his mother once so aptly put it.' It was certainly a turbulent time for her, though.

Amidst the chaos created by the selling of her story, Diana gave birth to her first child. On 4 February 1960, after a labour lasting twenty-seven hours, she and Dawson had a son, Mark Richard. Despite a somewhat traumatic birth, Diana instantly loved him with all her heart and felt an amazing sense of contentment and relief. However, it was soon back to work for her, and within a month of baby Mark's arrival, her agent and Dawson were negotiating a contract for her to appear in Las Vegas. She would need to accept the fact that she would be a working mum.

Early 1960 also saw the release of her first and only studio album. She had impressed audiences with her singing voice as part of her cabaret shows, and *Swingin' Dors* showed off her talent with a number of swing music numbers arranged by band leader, Wally Stott. The record was released by Pye, on tinted pink vinyl, with a lavish gatefold cover. The songs suited her range, and befitted her own story of fun romances, lost loves and dodgy men. As writer Damon Wise suggests, the inclusion of the song 'Come by Sunday' was perhaps a tongue-in-cheek reference to her own dislike of the dreary Sunday afternoons of her childhood and the visits to her grandma.

Diana's film career had been on the wane, even before selling her life story and the negative coverage it garnered. She had fallen far, from the heights of high-fee cabaret appearances in glamorous resorts, to the working men's clubs of northern England. A possible biopic of her rise to fame that had been touted was apparently now off the table too. She knew she could not afford to be too choosy when it came to the film roles offered to her.

However, she decided against one role that apparently came her way, much to her cost artistically. In her autobiography, she recalls being offered a lead role in *Saturday Night and Sunday Morning*, the adaptation of the Alan Sillitoe novel which went on to be an influential film of the British New Wave, defining a new and exciting era in cinema. It was playing opposite a young Albert Finney, but the part of married woman Brenda, who has an affair with the callous Arthur Seaton, called for the character to attempt a back-street abortion. The thought apparently horrified Diana due to her embarrassment at the subject matter – she had been under contract to the strict and proper Rank Organisation for many years, after all – but also perhaps due to her own experience a few years previously.

Saturday Night and Sunday Morning (1960), directed by Karel Reisz, was to become a defining film of the 1960s, and taking on the role could have restored her reputation as a dramatic actress. Yet her agent turned it down, mainly due to the lack of money on offer rather than any artistic doubts. The part eventually went to Rachel Roberts, whose critically lauded performance garnered awards and praise, and became a jewel in her respected film career. She also went on to star memorably in *This Sporting Life* (1963) opposite Richard Harris.

Diana reflected on the decision, acknowledging that the role could have rejuvenated her professional reputation and regained some of the excitement around her that she achieved with *Yield to the Night*. It also would have helped to lift her out of what she referred to as the 'social abyss into which the newspaper serial had plunged me'. Other accounts of the reasons she did not land the role vary, but the offer had been made and it could have all been so different.

She was aware that the 1960s shift in cinematic style meant a change in the perception and portrayal of women on screen, and the effects it could have on her career. Later, in 1966, she reflected in the *Sunday Express*, 'One has to play it cool to be fashionable. The Julie Christie kooky dolly look is all the rage now…The luxury and glamour that was once part and parcel of being a film star is now passé.'

Diana did go on to appear in a realist-style film in 1963, although it does not form part of the official British New Wave canon. *West 11*, a crime drama directed by Michael Winner and starring Alfred Lynch, Kathleen Breck and Eric Portman, was based on Laura Del-Rivo's debut 1961 novel *The Furnished Room* and was adapted for the screen by Willis Hall and Keith Waterhouse. Filmed on location around Notting Hill's seedy jazz clubs, coffee bars and bedsits, it tells the story of a young misfit and drifter called Joe Beckett, played by Alfred Lynch, who becomes involved with a plot to murder a wealthy old lady. Diana plays Georgia, a slightly older member of the group of local residents who Joe spends his time with. Joe seemingly takes advantage of Georgia's friendship and her loneliness.

Although not considered a classic, the on-location camerawork of cinematographer Otto Heller captures the shabby, squalid Regency houses that filled the area, which, with echoes of the infamous London landlord Rachman, were peddled for extortionate rents. One critic noted at the time in *Variety*, 'It has its merits. The sleazy London locations are very authentically shown. Perhaps too authentically.'

Diana was set to appear in cabaret at The Dunes hotel in Las Vegas for a month. She was unhappy at the thought of leaving Mark behind but found a nurse to care for him. The increasingly close bond between the nurse, Amy Brennan, and her children would become a recurring worry for Diana through the years.

In Vegas, Diana performed in the heat, three shows a night and seven nights a week. It was a relentless schedule. She lived a nocturnal life, performing until 4 am, then sleeping in the daytime before the early evening performance. She hardly saw her husband, who was often gambling in the casinos. She was missing her son, and was homesick and exhausted.

There was one highlight, however, as Mark was brought over as a surprise. This really lifted Diana's spirits: 'My joy was indescribable, and the knowledge that they were going to stay for the rest of my engagement made me a stronger, happier woman.' But instead of heading home after the end of her Las Vegas run, Diana was convinced to instead sign a contract to appear at a twice-nightly cabaret at Lake Tahoe. Dawson loved it in America, almost as much as Diana disliked it. After that ended, they headed to Hollywood and a two-week appearance at a nightclub, Ciro's.

Despite her wish to return home to the UK, the engagement at Ciro's had apparently caused quite a stir in entertainment circles. Offers of roles started to trickle in once again in films such as *The Ladies Man* (1961) with Jerry Lewis, and *On the Double* (1961) with Danny Kaye, who plays two roles in the film: an American soldier and a British general. However, when she agreed to appear as Sergeant Bridget Stanhope in *On the Double*, she was subsequently replaced in *The Ladies Man* by another actress, Pat Stanley. She still received her fee, though.

That year also saw her appear in *The Big Bankroll* (1961), an American crime biopic which was also known by the alternative title, *King of the Roaring 20s: The Story of Arnold Rothstein*. Set during the American Prohibition era, it stars David Janssen, Dianne Foster and Jack Carson.

The film tells the story of gangster Arnold Rothstein, who became a major figure in the criminal underworld. Diana plays Madge, a character based on Peggy Hopkins Joyce, who was an actress, artist's model and dancer at the time. Joyce herself had a rather flamboyant and controversial lifestyle. She married six times and had a number of scandalous affairs with very wealthy men. Like other real-life people depicted in the film, Joyce did not give permission for her name to be used, therefore Diana's character was retitled.

The Big Bankroll was based on a bestselling book by Leo Katcher, a screenwriter, author and journalist who, as West Coast Correspondent for the *New York Post* in 1952, helped to break the story about the then Senator Richard Nixon's election expenses in his campaign to run for Vice-President, which provoked him into making a famous televised defence. The film was the latest in a long line of gangster-themed films made by Allied Artists, including the successful *Al Capone* (1959) and *The George Raft Story* (1961).

All was not well on the domestic front, however, as Diana's relationship with Dawson continued to feel the strain, 'I was becoming aware of the intensity of his ambition, which became more and more determined as I went from strength to strength professionally.' Diana also suffered the impact of his mood swings. He was not prone to violent rages like Hamilton, which despite their intensity were at least over and done within minutes. Dawson instead would give Diana the silent treatment, 'With Dickie it was like a cold war; days of silence would pass between us and were much more damaging to our relationship than any physical violence.' She wondered where his spark had gone, thinking perhaps he was disappointed that he had not been the overnight success as a comedian that he had hoped.

Fuelled perhaps by the knowledge that a return to Britain would mean facing bankruptcy, Diana relented and agreed to stay in the US. Her career prospects seemed good over there and work was ticking along nicely again. On advice, they sold their home in Virginia Water and bought a property in Beverly Hills, vacating the rented mansion they had been staying in that had once belonged to Greta Garbo. Dawson was delighted. Still focused on making a career there himself, the couple hardly spent any time together. While Hamilton had revelled in standing in her shadow and being referred to as 'Mr Dors', Dawson did not appreciate the same lack of status. At parties, he followed his own path to mingle with the right people, leaving Diana to her own devices. He apparently criticised her way of dressing, referring to the figure-hugging dresses and low necklines she was known for as tarty. There was beginning to be an almost unbearable atmosphere at home. This was not helped by his apparent lack of money management skills; according to Diana, he would often make extravagant purchases which worried her. She had been there before with Hamilton.

During her time in the US, Diana also filmed two Alfred Hitchcock television films. She starred in 'The Sorcerer's Apprentice', an episode of *Alfred Hitchcock Presents* in 1962. Written by Robert Bloch, who wrote the novel *Psycho*, Diana starred as Irene Sandini, the wife of a carnival magician, The Great Sandini. After she helps him, a young man becomes infatuated with her. She decides to murder her husband and frame the young man for the crime. The half-hour episode was not screened by NBC at the time, as its ending was deemed too gruesome for broadcast and risked frightening the sponsors. But it was later screened when the series was syndicated to various channels, and included in a number of Hitchcock anthologies. Despite its controversial history, it has become one of the most watched *Alfred Hitchcock Presents* episodes, and due to its lapsed copyright and public domain status, it is also available to view online as part of the American Digital Library. Diana also recorded an episode for *The Alfred Hitchcock Hour*, the series which followed *Alfred Hitchcock Presents*. The episode, entitled 'Run for Doom', was broadcast in 1963, and Diana plays a nightclub hostess who marries a young doctor, is unfaithful, and then gets more than she bargained for when she decides to leave both her husband and her lover.

After feeling that the strain between herself and Dawson was becoming intolerable, and living in misery at home, Diana found comfort in the arms of another man. She began an affair with young actor John Ashley, whom she met on the set of television series, *The Racers*. When Dawson flew back to the UK to deal with some financial issues, Diana and Ashley's romance blossomed even more. He was apparently smitten and begged her to get a divorce from Dawson, but Diana refused to abandon her marriage for what she thought might just be an infatuation. One evening, however, they came home to Diana's house after a date to discover Dawson sat waiting for them. Things inevitably came to a head with Dawson. They discussed divorce, but Diana headed off on a three-week cabaret tour of South America with matters unresolved. When she returned, there was a showdown between Dawson and Ashley. Without going into detail, Diana recalls the incident in her 1981 autobiography and indicates that Ashley's behaviour was unacceptable. She finished the relationship, and she and Dawson attempted to mend their broken marriage.

In 1961, Diana returned to London to appear in cabaret. She was delighted to be back home for a while but, whilst there, she was completing the residency application forms for the US. It was during that time she discovered that Dawson had not been telling her the whole truth about his personal history, particularly his parentage. On his form he had written in the names of his aunt and uncle in Gosport, Hampshire. Dawson avoided her questions on the subject.

Diana stayed on in London due to filming commitments, so she rented a house. Mark was already with her but Dawson flew back from the US at Christmas, just in time for Diana to reveal to him that she was expecting their second child.

Her happiness almost turned to tragedy, however. While she was in the early stages of her pregnancy at a busy Bonfire Night party at the Buckinghamshire home of showbusiness agent John Kennedy, someone threw a firework into the house. It ignited a box of fireworks, exploded and caused a house fire. Diana was forced to climb out of a window to escape, but it was reported that two people lost their lives in the fire and another died from a heart attack. Diana claimed in her autobiography that she jumped from the window into the arms of her ex-boyfriend Tommy Yeardye, who also helped other people escape from the house.

After the drama of the Bonfire Night incident and completing her latest cabaret stint in London, Diana travelled back to the US to prepare for the birth of her second child. On 27 June 1962, Diana and Dawson's second son, Gary was born. Older son Mark, now two and a half, was thrilled to have a brother. However, again within weeks of the birth, Diana was back at work performing in yet another cabaret show, this time in Chicago. This was swiftly followed by another engagement in Las Vegas. Back home in Beverly Hills, her marriage was showing further signs of strain. Dawson's parents, whom Diana had only recently met, came to stay with them for a year. Diana was delighted to have the company as Dawson was still locking himself away from the rest of the family. However, having secured himself an agent, Dawson's own career started to show some progress and he made a handful of TV appearances. Diana dared to hope this might do the trick.

That year, 1962, also saw the release of the British comedy film *Mrs Gibbons' Boys*, which Diana appeared in as Myra. Based on a play by Joseph Stein and Will Glickman, and directed by Max Varnel, the little-seen film stars Kathleen Harrison, Lionel Jeffries and John Le Mesurier. A widow (Harrison) finally finds love and happiness, only to find everything thrown into disarray when her two wayward sons escape from prison and beg her to hide them. It was apparently released in the UK as the second half of a double bill with historical drama *Constantine and the Cross* (1961), which must have made for rather an odd cinematic combination. The film played once again on Diana's daring, sexy image. One poster advertising the film had a large image of Diana in a saucy-looking black slip, describing her as 'guest star Miss Diana Dors' and emblazoned across the top, 'Diana Dors is back…sizzling!' This must have been a bit of a disappointment to the lead stars.

In April 1963, when Diana was appearing in cabaret in New York, she received a call to say that her father had passed away. This inevitable news – he had not been well the last time she had seen him – left Diana with mixed emotions. After all, she had spent her whole youth expecting him to die before his time like he always said he would. Yet he outlived her mother by several years. Diana recalled that she did not feel shocked by the news, and did not cry or have the same intensity of response that she had felt with her mother's death. Despite a growing feeling of respect for him over the years as she got older, she had never felt close to her father. She spoke to her father's wife, her Aunty Kit, and was told he died in his sleep and did not suffer. Diana chose not to return home for the funeral.

After a few weeks, Diana returned alone to the east coast to appear in a production of George Abbott and Richard Bissell's stage musical,

The Pajama Game at the Meadowbank Theatre in New Jersey. She stayed for the whole summer. She felt that was the pattern for her now: weeks working away from her family, followed by a short reunion and then another trip away. Diana yearned to see her two sons. She also yearned for love and affection and found it in the arms of another man during that summer season in New York, a handsome, wealthy nightclub owner. What followed was a rather convoluted affair according to Diana. Frankie Jacklone was an insistent man who would not give up in his pursuit of her, despite it only being a summer flirtation from Diana's point of view.

Diana prepared for a long trip to Australia to perform a cabaret tour. She was dreading it, and not looking forward to another two months away from her boys. She knew nobody over there and thought she would suffer terrible loneliness. It played horribly on her mind. She still did not know how to feel about her crumbling marriage, or what would become of it, describing her and Dawson as being 'neither friends nor lovers'. She felt there was no progress with her brooding husband; they were just being torn further and further apart each time she left for work. She also knew that there would be other John Ashleys as she was a woman with needs, 'I was a woman who needed the attention of men, desiring the compliments they paid and the affection they bestowed. Especially as I never received them from the man I married, for better or worse.' There was no sign of a reconciliation, and the marriage felt an even lonelier prospect than the trip to Australia.

Chapter 8

A New Frontier

In the autumn of 1963, Diana reluctantly travelled out to Australia with a sinking feeling in her stomach. Arriving in Sydney after a gruelling eighteen-hour flight, she still had to endure another six-hour flight to Perth where the tour was starting. She described feeling a deep sense of despair at the prospect of the tour, and the mess she was leaving behind at home. She was hardly in the mood for the welcoming party that greeted her on arrival at Perth airport, which included the press, soldiers on parade, a brass band and a motorcycle escort. She put on a smile and posed for photos at the insistence of the tour manager, Jack Neary. She just wanted to go to her hotel and sleep. Before Neary would let her, he introduced her to one of the singers set to appear in her show. Despite Darryl Stewart being young and extremely handsome, Diana was in no mood to appreciate him.

Things were rather different the next day after a twelve-hour sleep, however, and Diana noticed him a great deal during the preparations for the show. As she stood in the wings on opening night and heard him sing, she felt a similar feeling to the early days with Dawson, watching him revel in the applause of the crowd. That evening they dined and laughed together, with Diana feeling a lightness that had eluded her for so long. She felt her mood transform over the next few days, helped by the endless summer sunshine. The hot days turned into balmy nights, and as Diana recalled, 'As moonlight bathed the Indian Ocean in silver, Darryl and I became more enchanted with the spell of each other.'

Stewart was also married with two young children, and any thoughts of long-term romance were soon tempered by consideration of the impact it would have. Diana's tour moved on to Sydney, and despite that being his hometown, Stewart was appearing elsewhere so they parted company. For now. In Sydney, Diana rented a penthouse suite and assumed full-on party hostess mode, spending time with the other stars appearing in cabaret in the city. When Stewart arrived back in town, they resumed their affair, the forbidden nature of it replacing the freedom they'd had in Perth but giving it an extra frisson.

As Christmas approached, Diana's time in Australia was over and she faced the prospect of leaving Stewart and returning home. The trepidation she had felt about her time in Australia had been replaced by a feeling of joy and satisfaction. She was popular there, a little too popular in some people's eyes. One rather hysterical woman at a show in Sydney apparently threatened to divorce her husband due to his interest in Diana, and was quoted as saying, 'He brought me to see Nelson Eddy…but he says now he's coming to watch That Sex Siren.'

The Australian media had been largely supportive in their coverage of her trip, with one journalist referring to her as 'Just plain Woman, intelligent, down-to-earth, contented with her life,' and complimenting her 'unusual honesty'.

Diana dreaded saying goodbye to Stewart, but she was taken aback when he announced he was coming to America with her. It was a wild and dangerous idea but Diana was delighted. A stopover in Hawaii before returning to Los Angeles was idyllic. Diana did not want it to end but knew she was just putting off the inevitable, and she returned home to Dawson and the children.

For a time, Diana continued to see Stewart in secret, grabbing precious time together whenever they could. But then disaster struck. Dawson received a letter from Stewart's wife, telling him all about the affair and revealing she was expecting another child. Diana and Stewart were unaware of the letter and the explosion awaiting them. In her 1981 autobiography, she recalled the showdown with Dawson. As she and Stewart headed out together for a drive, she spotted Dawson's car following them. There was the inevitable confrontation when they arrived outside Stewart's apartment, with Dawson telling her to leave the family home.

Diana sought legal guidance and was apparently advised to ask Dawson to leave the marital home, which she assumed she owned as she was making what she thought were regular mortgage payments. When asked how much money there was in their joint bank account, she admitted to there being just $1,500: hardly the amount expected for a successful film star. She was concerned that Dawson would take advantage and keep her out of the family home for good, and away from their boys. Discussions with Dawson ebbed and flowed, with suggestions of her withdrawing divorce proceedings and him remaining in the house, and it seems she relented.

Diana felt that she could not trust Stewart, even though he had left his pregnant wife in Australia to chase her halfway around the world. It left her with an empty feeling, a lack of trust and little confidence that they could make a future together after all. She was offered a play in Chicago, *Miranda*, a part she had played before as a young actress. She happily took the opportunity to get away from her troubles. Yet despite having doubts about him, Stewart eventually joined her in Chicago and they spent a few happy weeks together as a couple. But she knew with some regret that it was only temporary. Stewart flew back to Australia for the imminent birth of his child. They talked about meeting again when things had calmed down. She was scheduled to appear in a low-budget film back in the UK, *Allez France!*, so they arranged to spend the summer of 1964 together there. They shared their hopes for the future, exchanging promises and claiming undying love for each other. They wrote to each other obsessively, and even talked of getting married eventually. Not that Dawson would budge when it came to discussions of divorce.

The film itself was a French comedy of farcical misunderstanding and mistaken identity, co-directed by Robert Dhéry and Pierre Tchernia. Released in 1964 and also known as *The Counterfeit Constable* in English, it stars Dhéry, Ronald Fraser and Arthur Mullard, and concerns a French rugby supporter who is mistaken for a police officer on a trip to London. He becomes involved with a British movie star, played by Diana as herself. It was an interesting proposition, playing a version of herself on screen, and evidence of her burgeoning status as a British icon.

Before she started filming *Allez France!*, Diana was booked to do a six-week nightclub tour in England. Thanks to the Betting and Gambling Act of 1960, gambling was now legal, and casinos and nightclubs were popping up everywhere. Nightclubs were no longer just the preserve of the wealthy and were increasing in popularity. The success of the post-war coffee bars with their daytime dancing was on the wane, as many started frequenting their local clubs and discotheques. This meant there were now more opportunities for star names to perform in cabaret. The irony of Stewart continuing to bombard her with love letters while also talking about the birth of his new daughter with his wife was not lost on Diana, and she suspected they were reconciled. She endured a lonely time when working away from London, but made the most of being back home when she was in the capital. She spent time with her old friend, Michael Caborn-Waterfield, who was now engaged. But she still hoped that Stewart would be joining her there. Contact with Dawson was still very difficult; on her return trips home to see the boys, their relationship was strained but she endured it to spend the brief time she had with her sons. She recalled it was a very unhappy period for her, 'The pattern was so familiar now; all of us at the airport…and the boys saying their sad goodbyes.' But no matter how much she hated leaving her boys, the thought of spending time with Stewart when he came to London kept her going.

In London, she rented a cottage in Chelsea and filmed a TV play whilst awaiting the imminent arrival of her beloved Stewart. Except he never came. He wrote to say he could not come just now, but would try to do so in the future. Diana was devastated. Angry and upset, she sent a letter back, in which she demanded that he leave his wife and come at once. He did not, and she would not see him again for many years. Yet on the very same evening that she sent her impassioned letter to Stewart, she met another man at a party, and started another ill-fated romance with a dark-eyed, moody, young man with the improbable name of Troy Dante. There was an immediate spark between them, and a rather passionate and exhilarating romance, full of heated arguments and the fun of making it up to each other again. As Diana recalled, 'Troy brought out the worst in me, and there was no doubt that I did the same for him.'

Diana went to Paris to film for *Allez France!*, leaving Dante behind. Absence made the heart grow fonder, and their reconciliation on her return reignited the spark between them. By this point, her friend Michael Caborn-Waterfield's wedding was off, and she consoled him at his house in Dorset. Dante arrived to spend the weekend with her, but confessed he was married. Yet instead of listening to the warning bells about being involved with another married man, Diana asked him to move in with her in Chelsea. Theirs was a tumultuous relationship, peppered with what Diana simply referred to as their 'daily fight'.

The Swinging Sixties were well under way, and Diana's relationship with Dante fitted that hedonistic atmosphere perfectly. Theirs was a life of parties and enjoying the social life that London had to offer. She apparently even made claims to the press that she was going to manage Dante's pop career, much to their amusement. At this time, her career seemed to exist solely on cabaret turns and tours of northern clubs. They paid well and, as she had her family back home in Hollywood and her life with Dante to finance, she had to keep accepting those gigs. After all, her film career was not progressing. Diana, by her own admission, had started drinking heavily, which was very unusual for her, and she relied on her social life to keep her going. She started to resent paid work away from London as it would mean missing out on seeing friends and going to parties, despite the fact that it was her only income.

Diana hated the nature of the work she was getting: visiting working men's clubs in what she referred to as 'dreary northern towns'. There was no comparison with the life she had once lived, appearing for weeks in grand hotels in Las Vegas. She describes the venues as, 'Austere buildings with fluorescent lighting, Formica tables and audiences of men heckling me over their pints of beer. I was now prostituting my talent; peddling a screen name that had once been big…it seemed the only way left to earn a living.'

Not wanting to leave Dante, the only source of happiness in her life at the time, she stayed on in the UK and signed to appear in pantomime in Bromley, Kent. She was set to play the principal boy in *Sleeping Beauty*. She flew back to America to spend time with her sons, desperate to take them back to England with her when she left, but resigned to the feeling they were better off in Hollywood with the warmth and stability of the family home, rather than the procession of hotel rooms in cold British towns that had become her life now.

Back in London, Diana and Dante moved to a new flat on the King's Road, heading back into the world she had lived in early in her film career and with just as active a social life. Life went on in the same fashion she had become accustomed to, with endless parties, Dante gambling too much of her money, and heated arguments. His wife even showed up at one stage, angrily confronting them both about their affair. Yet despite the drama, Diana continued to want to be with him at all costs and by her own admission, showed not a thread of common sense where he was concerned. She even took him with her when she returned to America, squirrelling him away in a hotel while she returned home to see the boys, then dragging him across the country with her to appear in cabaret yet again.

Tour after tour, country after country, Diana travelled the often bleak cabaret circuit with Dante in tow. She even played a tour of American Army bases in Germany, performing in makeshift clubs on site, while drunk soldiers threw beer cans on the floor. She hardly felt appreciated for her art any more, and she was tired of trading on her faded sex symbol screen image. As she commented to an Australian magazine in 1963, 'Humphrey Bogart once said actors owe the public a good performance – they don't owe them anything more. He was so right. If you are typed as a sex symbol and play this role in a movie and give a good performance, that's as far as it should go – to attempt to carry it into your private life is real nonsense.' Yet here she was being treated as nothing more than a glorified pin-up on stage by audiences with expectations.

An acting opportunity came up back in America, performing in a production of Kurt Weill's musical, *One Touch of Venus* at the Meadowbank Theatre in New Jersey where she had played in *The Pajama Game* some years previously. It was a two-month run and inevitably, she took Dante with her. While she appeared each night at the theatre, Dante remained in the hotel room, probably so he would not gamble. As well as financing their stay on the east coast, Diana recalled that she was still sending most of her earnings back home to Hollywood to support Dawson and the boys. However, Dawson apparently invested in a boat and fancy cars during that time, which rather confused Diana when he pleaded poverty.

The endless travelling between the UK and America to appear in clubs and being constantly away from her sons was an eternal torment for Diana, and she was also struggling to find the happiness she so desperately craved with Dante. Eventually, he ended their relationship to return to his wife, although that did not last long. He pleaded with Diana to take him back, even apparently suggesting the three of them live together. Diana resisted that offer but did take him back on a promise that he would quit his gambling and get a proper job. Blinded by her desperate pursuit of happiness, Diana was treading a seemingly endless path to misery and destruction.

When her London agent quit, Diana was faced with having to secure work show by show, taking jobs in northern clubs and sending any money she made back home to Dawson. But soon after this low point, he finally found paid work in America, appearing in what was to become a very successful television show, *Hogan's Heroes*. The CBS sitcom, which would run for six seasons from 1965 to 1971, was set in a German prisoner of war (POW) camp during the Second World War, and featured a group of American servicemen from the Air Forces, led by Colonel Robert Hogan (Bob Crane). Dawson starred as Corporal Peter Newkirk, the group's resident conman and safe-cracker, who also happened to be a skilled tailor and was put in charge of making uniforms for POWs to impersonate high-ranking German officials. It was the making of Dawson's celebrity career and he would go on to become a successful television star, with regular appearances on various panel shows and comedy sketch programmes, before finding huge success again as the host of the game show, *Family Feud* in 1976. He was also a regular guest host on the *Tonight Show* in the late 1970s, stepping in for Johnny Carson a number of times.

While Dawson started to climb the ladder of success in Hollywood, Diana's career was falling to new depths in the UK. She turned again to pantomime when the other offers ran dry. 1966 saw the release of the ensemble comedy film, *The Sandwich Man* starring Michael Bentine, in which she had a small role alongside many well-known British character comedy faces, including Terry-Thomas, Dora Bryan, Norman Wisdom and Harry H. Corbett. But further film roles were not always forthcoming.

In autumn 1966, filming began on *Berserk!* (1967), a British horror starring Joan Crawford, Ty Hardin and Judy Geeson. It is a rather macabre mother-daughter relationship thriller about a circus plagued with murders. *Berserk!* was Crawford's second-to-last film. Crawford stars as

Monica Rivers, who co-owns a circus and acts as its ring mistress. A series of gruesome murders amongst the circus company puts Monica under suspicion. Diana appears as Matilda, a member of the circus company, who unsuccessfully attempts to seduce Ty Hardin's handsome tightrope walker, Hawkins, much to the dismay of jealous Monica. Crawford apparently enjoyed the experience of making the film and seemingly revelled in the colourful role. Diana enjoyed working with Crawford, admitting she was in awe of her, 'She was an incredible character, strange and puzzling, but whatever else a "superstar" in her profession!' Diana shared a few anecdotes about Crawford in her book, *Behind Closed Doors*. Apparently, when the British actor Michael Wilding asked Crawford if she ever watched the rushes from the previous day's filming, she responded that she did, but only once, 'Not to see myself, for I am always good…but to find out who else might be good, and make sure they never are again!'

There were happy times, however, and it was a great fillip that Christmas when the boys came over for a visit. 4-year-old Gary had never even set foot in the UK. Diana and her children enjoyed a wonderful Christmas, but when it came time to say goodbye, she was devastated. With little work on the horizon and the constant threat of bankruptcy hanging over her, she did not know when she would be able to travel to America to see them again. She again sought solace in her buoyant social life, revelling in hosting parties for her celebrity friends and various hangers-on. She and Dante made the most of it all, knowing it to be inevitably short-lived.

Diana was 35 years old and moving between rented places, but she desperately wanted to put down roots again. She saw a house she wanted to buy in Sunningdale near Windsor in Berkshire, yet with the constant shadow of the bankruptcy always in view, there was seemingly no way she could find the money. She sought advice from lawyers, and considered her position on the family house in Hollywood. Someone even advised she just sell the Hollywood mansion and simply pay her tax bill once and for all. The intricate web of money and property that had been weaved had her trapped like a fly. In the end, she agreed that Dawson could divorce her. After two years of separation, there was seemingly no argument against it. There was one stipulation: that he would assume ownership of the Hollywood house. In the UK, Diana's money men relented and allowed her to purchase her dream home, Orchard Manor, in Sunningdale with the money she had previously put in trust for the boys' future. At last she felt able to start afresh.

1967 saw the release of *Danger Route* (1967) in which Diana had a small role. The British spy film, directed by Seth Holt and starring Richard Johnson as secret agent Jonas Wilde, was seen by some as an attempt to cash in on the success of the James Bond films. Diana plays Rhoda Gooderich, a housekeeper seduced by Wilde during his assignment. Made by Amicus Productions, the film was plagued by production problems during filming, and was not a success at the box office.

Diana, at least, had another film assignment, *Hammerhead* (1968), shooting on location in Portugal. It is a British neo-noir thriller film directed by American filmmaker David Miller, and stars Vince Edwards, Judy Geeson and Peter Vaughan alongside Diana. Based on the 1964 novel by James Mayo, its plot concerns a criminal mastermind called Hammerhead (Vaughan) with a taste for expensive erotic art, who attempts to steal NATO secrets, with an American agent hot on his trail. Diana plays Kit, one of Hammerhead's mistresses.

Yet after filming finished, it was another return to cabaret work, with her fee rapidly declining even for that. It was 1968 and her life had a predictable pattern to it. Travelling for cabaret work, the occasional trip to the US to see the boys, then back home to Dante and their party lifestyle. Diana had a small role in *Baby Love* (1968) playing the mother of a troubled teenage girl. After her character takes her own life early on in the story, Diana mainly appears in flashback scenes without dialogue.

Eventually, the inevitable happened and her bankruptcy proceedings began. Diana endured daily trips to London, to sit in stuffy offices and hear the officials raking over her life in preparation for the courts. She faced the experience alone. The boys came over for the summer, a glimmer of hope amongst the tattered ruins of her career and financial affairs, but the holiday soon ended, and the boys went back home to Dawson. He had legal custody of Mark and Gary, and although she wished for them to be with her, it was highly unlikely Dawson would ever agree to that.

As the bankruptcy court date loomed, Diana's money finally ran out. At 36, she said that she did not have a penny to her name. She was also divorced from Dawson, which the press at that stage did not know. Yet she knew she had no future with Dante. He would always be a gambler, he was still married, and she did not trust him.

She was offered a role in a new television series for London Weekend Television called *The Inquisitors*. This was the first crime drama for LWT; in thirteen parts, it was to star Tony Selby and young, up-and-coming actor, Alan Lake. Diana was to appear in the pilot episode, 'The Peeling of Sweet P Lawrence', as a seasoned stripper called Sweet P, who refuses to give evidence when she witnesses a crime.

Lake apparently greeted the news of her guest spot with incredulity, 'Ah yes, Madam Tits and Lips,' was his response to the producer. This was evidence of her apparent reputation preceding her yet again. Arriving for rehearsals, he expected her to be a fussy diva, not the quiet and professional artist who greeted him in the rehearsal room. The director apparently saw fit to inform Diana of Lake's nickname for her, much to her amusement. The nickname would go on to become a running joke between them for many years.

Lake was just her type, with dark hair and dark eyes, and when they met there was an instant spark of chemistry between them like she had never felt before. A talented actor, intelligent and engaging, Diana said he was the sort of man she had been searching for her whole life. And at 27 years old, he was single. Diana could not believe it, remarking to him, 'But there must be some woman about to throw herself off a bridge because of you?' She knew immediately that romance was going to blossom. Lake also knew he had met someone special, apparently surprised at how down to earth and funny she was. On their second dinner date, Lake gave her an amethyst ring he had inherited from his uncle, saying he had always intended to give it to the woman he would marry. Despite only knowing each other for a few days, falling in love was inevitable. It was as if they had known each other all their lives.

Chapter 9

Loving Alan Lake

Diana told Troy Dante that she had met someone else and that their relationship was over. He did not fight it, and after four turbulent years together, they parted. Her new life with Alan Lake was sweet from the start, and she described being with him as like 'being on a magic carpet ride to paradise'. After years in the professional and personal doldrums, she had a chance to enjoy a fresh start, with somebody seemingly uncomplicated, who was going places, and not just to the nearest casino. Yet she inevitably wondered what would go wrong this time. Lake was nine years her junior, but at 37, she felt she deserved happiness with a man. Friends were concerned but she shrugged it off, instead joking about the age gap.

Just seven weeks after meeting, they got married. The brief wedding ceremony took place on 23 November 1968 at Caxton Hall, which with a tremendous splash of irony was where she had married Dennis Hamilton seventeen years previously. This time, however, things were very different. Diana wore a white lace dress, while the groom donned a black velvet suit. They had friends and family in attendance, and dozens of press photographers. The wedding was followed by a glitzy champagne reception at a London club. When asked why he had married Diana, Lake quipped that it 'wasn't for her money'.

Sadly for Diana, her boys were not in attendance. She claimed that Dawson had not even told them they were divorced, let alone that she was remarrying. But she was happy, and this time she did not have the doubts on her wedding day that she had felt previously.

Lake was not without his complexities, of course. Handsome and talented, he was also headstrong and impetuous, and gained a bit of a reputation during his time at the Royal Academy of Dramatic Art (RADA), as much for his heavy drinking as his acting potential. Diana described him as being a typical artist: temperamental with an explosive temper. It has been suggested that some of her close friends disapproved of Lake and worried for Diana. They apparently could see that he loved her deeply, but they did not want her with another Dennis Hamilton, causing trouble for her with erratic behaviour. But Diana and Lake were completely enamoured with each other. Her friend Bob Monkhouse later commented, 'Their devotion to one another was profound.' Lake was passionate and abundantly energetic, which Diana sometimes found rather exhausting. But she also claimed he was a deeply shy man, sensitive, truthful and above all, kind in nature. Diana was enchanted by him.

Following the pattern of swiftness they had established early on, Diana and Lake were soon expecting their first baby together. She worried that at 37 she was a bit old to have another child, and that it was too soon in the relationship to be concerned with domestic matters, rather than being focused on their love for each other. But she put the concerns about the honeymoon being over too quickly aside and focused on the future. Lake was, unlike the other men in her life, a hard-working man. He was a rising star, always working, and as a result he built his acting reputation. Sadly, *The Inquisitors*, the show which had led to their first meeting, never aired. With just three of the planned thirteen episodes filmed, including the one with Diana, the series was shelved without apparent explanation. However, some of the scripts are now held in the British Film Institute Reuben Library.

Lake was not earning film star fees yet he provided the money, giving Diana an opportunity to stop working while she was pregnant, something she had not had the luxury of with Mark or Gary, as she had always been the one having to earn. She was yet again horribly sick during the pregnancy, but their son Jason was born on 11 September 1969 without any complications, and they set about being parents together.

With Lake's career on the ascendant, Diana was happy to be at home 'playing the part' of a wife and mother. She even courted the press with her new domesticated image, sharing recipes and presenting herself as a Mother Earth figure. She felt perfectly content for the first time in her adult life. But when Lake was offered a role in the comedy, *Three Months Gone* by Donald Howarth at the Royal Court Theatre, the producer asked

Diana to read the script too. She was not overly keen on the idea of a return to work, or the part she was offered as a sex-crazed landlady. But Lake was to play one of her lodgers, and it offered them the chance to enjoy some funny scenes together, so she was eventually persuaded.

As Christmas 1969 approached, Diana persuaded Dawson to let Mark and Gary come over to visit. She had not seen them for almost two years at that stage, and she was desperate for them to meet Lake and their new baby brother, Jason. He seemingly relented when she sent the money for the air fares. The two older boys apparently loved Lake and they were able to attend Jason's christening too.

Three Months Gone opened at the Royal Court on 28 January 1970 to great success. This was Diana's first opportunity to play a character role and she grabbed it with both hands, 'I knew that on opening night that all the critics were waiting for me, their pens dipped in vitriol, ready to scribble acid reviews.' It had been fifteen years since the success of *Yield to the Night*, with little but the disappointment of cabaret in working men's clubs, lukewarm film reviews and bankruptcy in between, and she was determined to prove her critics wrong. She was ready to show the world what she was capable of.

The irony of fame and fortune is that it can often turn on a sixpence. How quickly things can shift, the sweet smell of success replacing the stench of professional degradation and failure. The press had revelled in her has-been status and her fall from grace. From being the sex symbol of the moment and the toast of Hollywood to a showbusiness joke, they had tracked every mis-step. Their cries of 'Diana Dors can really act!' amused her greatly. As she commented, 'What better experience could an actress have had than the hell I'd been through in recent years?'

The play and the performances by Diana and Lake were critically acclaimed. *The Observer* said Diana had given an 'astonishingly masterful character performance'. The play transferred from the Royal Court to the Duchess Theatre for a long West End run. As well as the stability this offered her, it also led to other acting offers and her career felt buoyant again, with Diana commenting that it felt like she had a whole new career. Diana knew she needed to capitalise on the success of the play, 'I now have to be choosy if I'm not to undermine the good that was done by

Three Months Gone, which brought about some wonderful offers and a new recognition of the fact that I could act,' she told *Films and Filming* magazine in 1970. But yet again she was faced with a choice between critical acclaim and paying the bills, 'People soon forget, and if one accepts too many crappy parts, it becomes a case of "wasn't she in a good play – once?"…art all too seldom equals box office.'

However, as their professional lives both continued to blossom, Diana began to notice that Lake was drinking a great deal. She was used to dealing with drunk men in nightclubs and on the cabaret circuit, or friends over-indulging at parties, but this was different. To live with someone who needed alcohol every day was very difficult, and it worried her greatly. She did not understand alcoholism as an illness and did not know how to handle it. She had experienced the odd incident with him early on, but claimed that being blissfully in love meant she did not register the warning signs. There was an occasion when she was pregnant with Jason, for example, when Lake became drunk and took an overdose of pills. Yet Diana said she did not suspect alcoholism, putting it down to artistic overindulgence.

She came to understand the extremes of his behaviour, as he became something of a Jekyll and Hyde character. His moods would dominate their marriage. When he was sober, he was the gentle, intelligent, kind man she married. But when he drank, he became irritated and occasionally frightening. His reliance on alcohol never seemed to Diana to affect his acting performances, but she noticed that towards the end of *Three Months Gone*, he had taken to visiting the pub next door during the interval, throwing down drinks in rapid succession before carrying on. At that stage she still convinced herself he was just a heavy drinker, not a dependent drinker, just like many of the young men in need of the stimulation she encountered in the acting world. But he apparently got into trouble occasionally, with one particular altercation in a pub leading to a bruised hand and the need for his understudy to step in according to some accounts.

As the summer approached, Diana looked forward to Mark and Gary visiting from America. The play was nearing the end of its run and she hoped to spend lots of quality time with them, Lake and Jason. In her 1981 autobiography, Diana recalls that on one particular Sunday before the boys arrived, Diana's friend 'Leapy' Lee Graham and his wife came over to see her and Lake. Graham was an old friend of Diana's and was now enjoying a successful pop career with hits such as 'Little Arrows'. He and Lake got on well, and like on many other occasions, they went to the local pub for a few drinks while Diana and Graham's wife stayed in the house chatting. Lake and Graham drank heavily into the afternoon. An argument apparently broke out between the two drinkers and the stand-in landlord of the pub, followed by a fight with some locals which resulted in some injuries. The police were called, and Graham was charged with stabbing after using a penknife. Lake was charged with being an accessory and faced the prospect of being up in court.

Predictably, the incident was all over the newspapers. Diana's personal life had been largely publicity-free for a while, so returning to such a state of high alert on that front was a concern for her, especially with the boys arriving for the summer. Yet she enjoyed the time with them, despite the worry of Lake's court case hanging over them. As they left for home in the US, she knew that at least it would not be long before she saw them again. She and Lake had a holiday in the States planned, and as he was granted bail, he was still allowed to leave the country at least. It was Lake's first trip to the US, and as they spent time with the boys at Diana's old mansion, Dawson was very friendly. He was enjoying a lot of success and was actively dating, and they spent an enjoyable few weeks there.

Diana's relationship with the boys' long-term nanny Amy Brennan was still incredibly strained, and tensions between the two women had been building for many years. Amy had always doted on Diana's boys, having been in their lives since she became nurse to Mark in 1960 when he was a few months old. At first, Diana had been relieved to find a nurse who took such great care of her children but over the months and years, she became increasingly concerned about the influence she felt Brennan had over them, referring to her 'lies and fantasies'. This became a continued focus for Diana as the boys got older and contact with them became more sporadic. She felt that Brennan thought she did not care enough about her children and was turning them against her in her absence.

The tensions eventually reached breaking point when, in February 1974, Diana wrote a very personal article for *Woman's Own* magazine about Brennan and her concerns. She talked about her reasons for keeping Brennan on to care for her children, despite her worries. She also talked about the pressures of being a working mother and continually facing a life on the road performing in clubs when her career was flagging: 'Was this the life, then, to offer my sons? Should I have dragged them around the Northern towns where I worked, living in hotels, and in a cold-weather climate they weren't used to?' She also voiced her concerns about what her boys might think of her, suggesting they barely knew her and hoping that one day they might grow to love her. This outpouring in the press did not go down well with Brennan, and the two women did not manage to resolve their differences before Brennan's death in the summer of that year.

In 1970, on their return to the UK, Diana and Lake were both due to start work on a new television series called *Queenie's Castle*. Made by Yorkshire Television, it was set and filmed in Leeds. The show was written by Keith Waterhouse, a Leeds journalist and author of *Billy Liar* and other notable works, and Willis Hall, the Leeds playwright who adapted *Billy Liar* for the stage. The men were lifelong friends and creative collaborators. *Queenie's Castle* would eventually run for three successful series on ITV.

The series revolves around the Shepherd family, who live in Buckingham Flats, a sprawling social housing development in inner-city Leeds. Diana stars as the blowsy Queenie Shepherd, the family matriarch who rules her castle and her kingdom with gusto and takes no prisoners. She lives in her flat with her three feckless sons Raymond (Freddie Fletcher), Douglas (Barrie Rutter) and Bunny (Brian Marshal). The plot revolves around their various dodgy shenanigans and schemes, as they run rings around the residents and the police. It is a typical set-up echoed in many subsequent British sitcoms over the next couple of decades. Queenie's husband, Lionel never actually appears on screen and is usually referred to as working away in various locations, leaving viewers to assume he is probably banged up in prison. Queenie's wheeler-dealer brother-in-law, Jack (Tony Caunter) also lives with the family. Lynn Perry also stars as Queenie's nemesis, the chair of the Residents' Committee and general do-gooder, Mrs Petty.

Never officially referenced as the setting, although everyone knew it to be the case, the show used the famous Quarry Hill Flats in Leeds for its location shooting. Now long demolished, the flats were positioned high up on the city's skyline. Due to their positioning at the end of Eastgate, one of the city centre's main roads, the flats reminded the writers of The Mall and Buckingham Palace, hence the name of the show and the fictional estate. Built in an Art Deco style in the 1930s, Quarry Hill Flats were notable as the first council flats of their kind. Exteriors for *Queenie's Castle* were also shot around Leeds Market, much to the shock of the locals, with interiors filmed at Yorkshire Television studios down the road.

Diana gave a striking and warmly received performance in the lead role. Queenie is tough, but always has time for her friends if they need her. She is protective of her clan, though, and her sharp tongue would make her clash with others. In an interview with *TV Times*, Waterhouse and Hall suggested, 'It would be going too far to say that Queenie has a heart of gold. Perhaps a heart of brass would be nearer the mark.' Waterhouse and Hall wrote Queenie and her family sympathetically, but there is a spikiness to it that was unusual for a comfy mainstream sitcom at that time. They knew Leeds and its people, and they included the kind of eccentricities and local nuances in the characters that would resonate with, but not alienate, the audience. Diana always had a soft spot for Queenie Shepherd, and the show was a success and fondly remembered by many. As Diana later commented, 'Children particularly loved the character of Queenie, though heaven knows why, as she was always whacking her three sons with a handbag.'

Barrie Rutter, who played Douglas, one of Diana's sons in *Queenie's Castle*, recalls working on the show with affection. As a young northern-based actor at the time, he felt it was a great opportunity to work on a television show with a northern sensibility. Their ability to film external shots around the vast Quarry Hill Flats complex was slightly compromised though, 'We were always surrounded. We did not do a great deal of filming there because kids would wreck the tv vans and stuff, so much dropsy was given to the local tear-arses, we made them "security".' Interior filming was done at Yorkshire Television, and Rutter recalls that even the cast and crew from other shows loved to see Diana there and that it was quite an event, 'At the time she was really in her pomp. Everybody knew she was in the building and loved it.'

Rutter loved working with Diana on the show and they became lifelong friends, 'She was wonderful, I loved her to bits. She had a wonderful way with words, she was remarkable, a very intelligent woman.' They bonded over an interest in theatre and Rutter remembers many conversations about Shakespeare and classical theatre. *Queenie's Castle* was a very social show to work on and a day's filming would often end in the pub. But Rutter recalls that Diana did not need to drink alcohol to have a good evening out with her fellow cast and crew, 'I never saw her drink. She had a thimble full of champagne on her fortieth birthday. She never did drugs either, she was just high on life.'

But with his court case looming, there were doubts about Lake's role on the show. He was due to play the part of Queenie's brother-in-law. Barrie Rutter recalls that the initial read-through of the script with the cast took place with both Diana and Lake at their house in preparation for the upcoming start of filming. Diana recounted that Lake's lawyers suggested he plead guilty. As it was his first offence, they felt he was unlikely to get a custodial sentence and it would speed up proceedings. With a car literally waiting outside to speed them both up to Leeds, Lake awaited the verdict. It was terrible news, however. Graham got three years in prison and Lake was sentenced to eighteen months. It was their worst nightmare come true. Diana and Lake were allowed a quick goodbye before he was taken down to the cells and she was driven up to Yorkshire to begin filming without him.

Diana put on a brave face but felt utterly destroyed inside. On the first day of filming, she walked through Leeds Market while incredulous bystanders greeted her arrival in the city. But despite the brave smiles for onlookers, she was heartbroken to be there without Lake. Barrie Rutter also remembers her taking a very stoic approach to the situation, 'On the Friday he gets sent down, yet she did those opening shots in Leeds on the Saturday morning. She was a consummate professional.' Young Jason was being looked after by Lake's parents at least, which was a comfort to Diana. But she also recalled how heartbroken she was for them too. She simply kept going, feeling that nothing would be gained if she fell to pieces.

Diana visited Lake in Oxford Prison as often as she could, but the thought of him still being there at Christmas was devastating for them both. He was later moved to the island prison of Portland, near Weymouth in Dorset and the long drive to see him became a way of life for the next year. His appeal was turned down and the family faced up to the reality of it all. As Diana recalled, 'Our love, marriage and success, which had all started out so wonderfully, had been reduced to a three-hour meeting each month, sitting at a Formica-topped table in a miserable prison visiting room with other convicts' wives.'

On a brighter professional note, Diana's acting career had been revitalised and she kept working. She set off for the Almeria region in Spain to make *Hannie Caulder* (1971), a British Western directed by American Burt Kennedy, who was well known for many films in the genre in the US, working with John Wayne, James Garner, Robert Mitchum, Glenn Ford and Rita Hayworth. *Hannie Caulder* starred Raquel Welch as a frontier wife living at a horse station in the American West, who seeks revenge after her husband is murdered. It also features Robert Culp and Ernest Borgnine. Diana had a small cameo as a Madam. The film was not well received by critics at the time. Its mix of Western and horror elements, and the extreme violence, led to accusations of it lacking clarity, although it performed well at the box office. More recently it has been revisited by film critics, who have cited its importance as a step between the classic Westerns and the 1970s American independent filmmakers such as Sam Peckinpah and Sergio Leone. Director Quentin Tarantino said that the film was a big influence on his *Kill Bill* film series. After making *Hannie Caulder*, Kennedy directed a number of successful episodic American television shows.

Cabaret work was plentiful and Diana also filmed *Deep End* (1970). A US / West Germany co-production directed by Jerzy Skolimowski, *Deep End* stars Jane Asher and John Moulder Brown as two young co-workers at a suburban swimming pool and bath house in London. Moulder Brown plays Mike, a 15-year-old who gets a job at the local baths where he is trained by his co-worker Susan, played by Asher, who is ten years his senior. Their relationship has sexual undertones and Susan becomes the focus for Mike's lustful interest as he becomes infatuated with her. He discovers that his work at the baths also involves providing sexual gratification to customers. Diana plays an older client who gains sexual stimulation from pushing Mike's head into her bosom and talking about football suggestively, with references to George Best's performance on the pitch. 'He just pushed it in, just glided it in,' she fantasises aloud.

Her cameo performance as a demanding client was described by the film journalist Ryan Gilbey as a 'priceless incidental pleasure' within the film, 'This blonde typhoon in polka dots makes the bewildered hero an accessory to orgasm, clutching him to her bosom as she conducts aloud a George Best fantasy ("Tackle, dribble, dribble, score!").' The director Skolimowski recalled the wonderful experience of casting Diana in the film; her reaction to the ridiculous costume she had been asked to wear was to take it all in good humour and throw herself into the role. Talking a few years later, her co-star Moulder Brown remarked, 'In that scene with Di, she really bared her soul: this glamorous star suddenly allowed herself to be that vamping caricature.'

Deep End is considered to be unique and unusual, but also a charming and quirky film. The cast were asked to improvise as much as possible. Although it evokes such an atmospheric and realistic portrayal of London suburban life, the film was mainly shot in Munich, with locations in Soho and Leytonstone also used. The director Skolimowski is Polish, and the film perhaps benefits from having that feeling of an outsider's point of view of a very British setting.

Released in British cinemas in 1971, the film gained critical acclaim at the time but disappeared from circulation for many years and slipped from public attention, barely seen for decades due to rights issues. However, it was finally rescued from obscurity, digitally restored and re-issued by the British Film Institute for its fortieth anniversary in 2011 and gained recognition once again as a fascinating work of cinema. Although her appearance in the film was small, it brought Diana's acting talent to new audiences and paved the way for more nuanced and interesting roles in later years, 'I've got a chance of varied roles at my age, now that I'm not tied down to sex and glamour and vacuous romantic leads,' she told *The Guardian* in 1970.

Late 1970 saw the release of *There's a Girl in My Soup*, the romantic comedy film directed by Roy Boulting and starring Peter Sellers and Goldie Hawn, with Diana in a supporting role as a frumpy counterpart to the youthful Hawn character. It is based on the popular stage play by Terence Frisbee, which ran for six and a half years in the West End and was at the time London's longest-running stage comedy. The record was later surpassed by the critically panned farce, *No Sex Please, We're British*, which was subsequently made into a film in 1973, and then Ray Cooney's equally farcical *Run for Your Wife*. Adapted for the screen by Frisbee, *There's a Girl in My Soup* tells the story of vain, womanizing and wealthy television host, Robert Danvers, played by Sellers, who meets a straight-talking teenage American hippie called Marion, played by Hawn. Despite its beginnings as a slightly questionable British stage sex comedy, the film was critically acclaimed with reviewers describing it as 'a delightful surprise: a rather simple legit sex comedy...transformed into breezy and extremely tasteful screen fun,' and suggesting it was one of Sellers' best roles in years. Goldie Hawn was also praised for her performance and was nominated for a BAFTA for Best Actress.

Despite the precarious nature of her film career in the 1970s, Diana also took on a number of interesting television roles, carving out a niche for herself in character parts of the type she had predicted for herself back in the early 1960s. She demonstrated her wide acting range in a variety of television series.

In 1971, she appeared in a three-part adaptation of Shelagh Delaney's play, *A Taste of Honey* for the BBC. The production was aimed at schools and colleges as part of the channel's education output. Diana plays Helen, the mother of the main character, Jo, a role played in the 1961 film version by Dora Bryan. Helen is self-centred and has a drinking problem. She also has a complex relationship with her spirited daughter Jo, a role made famous by Rita Tushingham in the 1961 British New Wave Film of the play, directed by Tony Richardson.

Diana certainly kept busy professionally while she waited for her beloved Lake to be released from prison. She recalled that she felt so much love for him, in a way she had never experienced before. She was fully committed to him and their relationship. In honour of his upcoming release from prison after his eighteen-month sentence was reduced to twelve, Diana bought Lake a horse called Sapphire. As he returned home after his release on 16 October 1971 to be greeted by guests and well-wishers at the party she had arranged, she presented the horse to him, to his apparent delight.

As they started to look to the future, worries about Lake working again subsided as he signed up to appear in a television play alongside her. He seemingly gave a very professional performance, but away from the camera, time in prison had affected him greatly. He was not sleeping, and again he turned to drink for comfort.

One morning in early 1972, Diana received a shocking phone call. Lake had suffered a terrible fall from his horse while out riding in Windsor Great Park. He had been hit on the back by a tree branch. On arrival at hospital, the true extent of his injuries became clear. He had broken his back and shoulder in five places, and the doctors feared he would not walk again. But fortunately, after six weeks of bed-rest, he began to move again. There was a long road to full recovery ahead, but Diana was greatly heartened by the mental and physical strength he showed, determined to walk again and overcome the pain. It did not stop him drinking, however.

That year, 1972, as Lake focused on his physical recovery, Diana appeared in three films, including *Swedish Wildcats*, filmed in Copenhagen and directed by Joseph Sarno. The sexploitation film features Diana as Aunt Marghareta, the owner of a brothel. Diana also made *The Pied Piper* (1972), a film loosely based on the famous tale directed by Jacques Demy starring Jack Wild, Donald Pleasance and John Hurt, and also featuring an appearance by Donovan. Diana also featured in a film directed by her good friend, Lionel Jeffries, called *The Amazing Mr Blunden* (1972). The spooky family mystery is based on the novel *The Ghosts* by Antonia Barber, and tells the story of a Great War widow Mrs Allen (Dorothy Alison), who is forced to live in a squalid little Camden flat with her family. But after a visit from a mysterious old stranger, Mr Frederick Percival Blunden (Laurence Naismith), the family is given the opportunity to become the caretakers of Langley Park, a derelict country mansion in the Home Counties. The older children Lucy (Lynne Frederick) and Jamie (Garry Miller) see the ghostly figures of two children in the grounds, seemingly in need of their assistance. They have travelled from the past to warn of a terrible fate that threatens them. Lucy and Jamie set about helping them to escape their predicament by travelling back into the past with them. Diana plays Mrs Wickens who, with her husband (David Lodge), plots to kill the ghost children to get hold of their inheritance.

Lionel Jeffries had previously made the much-loved film version of *The Railway Children* (1970), and *The Amazing Mr Blunden* has been a nostalgic family favourite in Britain since its release. Lynne Frederick won the Evening Standard British Film Award for Best New Coming Actress in 1973 for her role in the film. Diana seemingly relished the opportunity to work with her friend Jeffries, but also to play such a wonderful character role as Mrs Wickens, which was described to her by Jeffries as 'a harridan'. Diana gives a delightfully wicked performance with a frightening intensity, and brings layers of camp and cartoon physicality to the role without ever falling into pantomime. It was very different to any role she had played before, and she worked hard to establish the grotesque character of Wickens. She delighted in the evilness of her and loved donning the make-up, including a horrible big wart on her nose. She was finally able to play a role where her looks did not matter.

Despite his slow recovery, Lake's drinking was continuing to affect their marriage. Diana feared his resentment at her career success while he was unable to work. The family holidays they managed to take were marred by booze and arguments. A trip to Canada, where Diana was appearing on a TV show, almost ended in disaster when his drunkenness meant she had to plead for him to be let on the plane to fly home. At home, his moods and excessive drinking led to arguments and confrontations. Lake's 'Mr Hyde' was dominating, concealing the wonderful man she had married. This ate away at their marriage, and she started to lose the respect and love she had for him. Recriminations would always follow, but promises to never again touch a drop were broken. Diana would often return home after filming to find him intoxicated, and she was losing the energy to attempt to reason with him about it.

While Lake returned to acting, Diana made another series of *Queenie's Castle*. This was followed by another show for Yorkshire Television, *All Our Saturdays*. Diana played Di Dawkins, the owner of a successful Yorkshire garment factory who unexpectedly inherits an amateur rugby league team. Not exactly top of the league, Di, or 'Big D' as she was known, tries to improve their fortunes. She even renames them the improbable 'Frilly Things'. Despite including Diana and some of her co-stars from *Queenie's Castle*, the show was poorly received by critics and never achieved the success of its predecessor; just six episodes were made and aired in 1973.

In spite of the premature ending of the successful *Queenie's Castle*, and the not so popular *All Our Saturdays*, Diana enjoyed the experience of working in television and was keen to do more. One option she was very keen to explore was presenting her own chat show, suggesting that it was the only artistic medium where you could truly be yourself. She knew from her cabaret shows that she was able to build a rapport with audiences very easily, as she was at ease with them and able to show her true personality between the songs and the impressions. Talking in an unpublished interview with journalist Ian Woodward, she confessed, 'I just feel that warmth coming from the audience when I stop performing and start being myself.'

That summer, her dream almost became a reality when she was given the opportunity to film a pilot for a pet chat show, the ingeniously titled *Paws for Dors*. Her guest stars were Dudley Moore, Zsa Zsa Gabor and the Marquis of Bath. Sadly, no series followed despite good audience ratings. The dream was on hold again for now.

The following year, 1973, saw Diana continue to appear in cabaret. She was performing near Wakefield when disaster struck: Diana tripped and broke her leg. She needed an operation to pin it, and was laid up in bed for three months as a result. Despite this mishap, she continued with filming commitments in Sweden. The producers were sympathetic to her predicament, apparently even suggesting she could play the part in a wheelchair.

In 1973, Diana appeared in the sitcom spin-off film, *Steptoe and Son Ride Again*. Directed by Peter Sykes and written by the original sitcom creators and writers, Ray Galton and Alan Simpson, it was the second Steptoe and Son spin-off, following on quickly from the eponymously named first film released the year before. The film starred Wilfrid Brambell and Harry H. Corbett, and saw Harold (Corbett) invest his father's life savings in a greyhound who is almost blind and can't actually see the hare. When the dog inevitably loses and Harold has to pay off the debt, he comes up with the idea of collecting his father's life insurance. But to do this, his father must pretend to be dead. Diana plays the nameless but rather shamelessly fruity 'Woman in Flat', who takes advantage of an unsuspecting Harold and makes a move on him. Dressed in a short leather skirt and long PVC boots, her character might not have been given a name, but she certainly made an impression.

Big screen versions of television programmes were a feature of British comedy cinema throughout the 1970s. Despite the reputation for quality comedy cinema in previous decades, including the charm and whimsy of the successful Ealing Comedies in the 1940s and 1950s, by the 1970s, the genre was well and truly tired. The British film industry's grasp on the kind of popular comedy that worked with audiences was faltering. Even the *Carry On…* films had become prosaic and were faltering by the middle of the decade, starting to mimic the more overt sexual representation found in the soft porn films that came to dominate, rather than the light-touch innuendo and vulgarity that had been its unique selling point.

British film comedy was now incredibly insular. The *Carry On…* films had never had much success with overseas markets, and this trend continued. If a filmmaker did not want to make a sexploitation film, the only option seemed to be a sitcom spin-off. As film journalist Julian Upton suggested, 'It was either a healthy pragmatism or a monumental lack of imagination that drove British film producers, in this newly "permissive" era, to the country's most conservative television culture – the half-hour sitcom – for material.' It was probably the latter, judging from the generally poor quality of the domestic comedy output that dominated cinemas in the UK in that period.

The sitcom has become a staple of British television and the 1970s is often seen as its golden age. The quality of the writing in shows such as *Steptoe and Son, Fawlty Towers, Porridge* and *Whatever Happened to the Likely Lads?* means their appeal has been enduring for audiences and cultural commentators alike. Even more mainstream, mass-appeal shows such as *On the Buses* and *Are You Being Served?* had big weekly audiences and people remain fond of them, despite the somewhat dated and often inappropriate lines and characters. The spin-off film was perhaps therefore seen as a safe bet. What could possibly go wrong?

Britain's domestic film industry needed this huge, conservative TV audience to visit their local cinemas in order to stay alive. The resulting output, however, varied considerably in quality from the original shows. A concept which worked in a television studio, and a setting that relied heavily on a sense of the small scale and the confines of a claustrophobic environment, faltered when let out into the big wide world. Some, such as *Porridge*, were well-crafted, bigger picture versions of their own formulas, with writing to match the comedic talents of the actors. Others failed to capture the magic they achieved on the small screen, despite the efforts of the acting and writing talent involved. Some were even weaker than their limited small-screen inspirations.

From the release of *On the Buses* in 1971 to *Rising Damp* in 1980, the sitcom big-screen outing dominated cinemas. Between 1968, when the big-screen version of *Till Death Do Us Part* was released, and 1980, over thirty feature films were made from successful sitcom origins. British film studios such as Hammer Films and British Lion felt obliged to contribute to the flurry of titles, perhaps just to see themselves through the trough in the domestic cinema market and hope to see it through the decade still functioning. Despite the lack of critical success, in most cases the films were popular with paying audiences. Reassuringly childish and rather smutty, many of them had the appeal of 'endearing but mischievous children'.

Many of the films in the spin-off genre focused on the usual television cast going away on holiday together. The trend started with the big-screen version of *Please, Sir* (1971) and was repeated in other subsequent films. It seemed that producers thought the premise of sending the characters out of their usual environment and into an awkward vacation scenario, usually abroad, and often the increasingly popular 'Costa Del Sitcom', was enough. In the first *Steptoe and Son* film released in 1972, the characters went to Spain. This was itself an echo of some of the popular films of the 1930s and 1940s, such as *Bank Holiday* and *Holiday Camp*, which Diana herself had appeared in. But now instead of making do with a trip to Butlins, the cast decamped abroad, mirroring the change in British society itself and the cheap all-inclusive holidays now within economic reach of the masses.

Eventually, as a new decade dawned, it would be the end of the road for the sitcom spin-off, and this also coincided with the end-point for a number of struggling film companies. In 1980, Hammer Films and British Lion had released their last film output, and the popularity of home video was about to have an impact on the film-viewing habits of UK audiences. Admissions were plummeting, cinemas were closing and in 1981, British cinema production reached an all-time low with just twenty-four films produced. A decade earlier, in 1971, the figure had been ninety-six. The end of the 1970s did not mark the end of the sitcom spin-off altogether though; as a genre, it has been revisited a number of times, again with variable success. There have been *Mr Bean* films, and *Absolutely Fabulous* had a successful outing on celluloid in 2016. *The Inbetweeners Movie*, based on the popular coming of age sitcom, was released in 2011. It was one of the most successful British films at the box office, setting a new record for the best box office opening weekend for a comedy film in the UK. Again, the cast went on holiday.

Diana's sexually dominant role in *Steptoe and Son Ride Again* seemed to fit perfectly with the way her image was developing into a kind of 'blowsy glamour', thanks in part to her own small-screen sitcom roles. In *Queenie's Castle* and *All Our Saturdays*, she had played sexually-confident Northern matriarchs using her female charms more overtly than in her youth, the confidence of her forties perhaps also coming into play. She was a mother, but she was also a self-assured woman. This change in image was noted in the press, their obsession with her changing body still dominating coverage of her acting career. One particularly snarky comment from a journalist described her as, 'All backless, strappy white high heels, fingers creaking under enough shiners to furnish a Bond Street jewellers – and eyelashes long enough to stir a Manhattan.'

In 1973, amongst the eclectic acting offers which ebbed and flowed, Diana received sad personal news. Her Aunty Kit had died from cancer and she was faced with the task of selling the family home. Her last connection with Swindon was gone. Around this time, Diana and Lake began developing an interest in Catholicism. Lake had begun seeking solace from his drinking in the Catholic church next door to their home, the peace and tranquillity offering him respite from his temptations. Diana shared that feeling too, and they felt that converting would be the right thing to do. Being divorced, however, made this a difficult step for Diana to take. But, after a year of devoted study and countless interviews with various clergy, in the spring of 1974, they were both accepted into the faith. They even took their marriage vows again, now in the eyes of God rather than just a registrar.

That summer, Diana was invited to play the role of Jocasta in a production of *Oedipus* at Chichester. This was a fantastic opportunity to display her classical acting mettle. It was her first real experience of performing classical theatre, and although she enjoyed it, Diana admitted afterwards that she also found the production exhausting. Newspaper reports at the time remarked on her bravery for taking on the role and doing something different, one headline describing her as 'The Indestructible Diana Dors'. She was apprehensive beforehand, but understood people's reaction to the choice of role, 'It's a long way from *Here Come the Huggetts* to Sophocles,' she remarked to one journalist, adding, 'Me in Greek tragedy, who'd have believed it? I suppose the only thing I haven't tried now is Billy Smart's Circus, and that will probably come in time.'

Diana admitted to being nervous beforehand. But she was delighted with her performance and said the experience was one of the greatest thrills of her life. Some theatre critics had suggested that it was a bizarre casting choice, but the opening night audience loved her and gave her the loudest applause of the night. In their reviews of the show, critics largely praised her performance, suggesting that she brought genuine humanity to the role. Reacting to the use of the word 'bizarre' to describe her casting in one newspaper, Diana said the critic had done her a favour as it made her so angry that she was determined to give an excellent performance to prove them wrong, 'If that man knew anything about Greek history he would realise I'm ideal. Queen Jocasta was a power-crazed nymphomaniac.'

Playing Jocasta was another turning point in her acting career and evidence of Diana feeling confident to take on different roles. Her age and reputation for glamour was now no barrier to taking risks and taking on a variety of parts, with more challenging work coming her way. But she would still face the same dilemma she always had: deciding between strong career choices and easier options for making money. She was well aware of the implications of both paths, but choosing her work wisely was not always an option for her as the decade progressed.

Chapter 10

The Swinging Mid-Seventies

By the mid-seventies, Diana was still finding she had to continue working the cabaret circuit. It was a steady income stream, but it surprised people when they realised she had a breadth of talent which included impressions and singing, commenting that often she felt the audience were thinking, 'Let's go and see old big boobs to see what she's really like.' It sometimes felt to Diana that she was almost prostituting herself. She knew she was a good actress and she just needed the chance to prove it, having spent years feeling the need to live down her blonde bombshell image. So, when she had been offered the role of Jocasta in *Oedipus*, she was delighted and hoped it would mean people would look to her acting ability, rather than only focus on her anatomy. It was also a chance to 'shock a few old ladies' too, which pleased her. But the more sophisticated roles still failed to materialise, and she found herself still working in television. She was seemingly happy with this, but it was not quite what she had hoped for after her positive press notices.

She appeared in another television play, as the lead in an episode of the ATV *Thriller* series. In the episode, 'Nurse Will Make It Better', she plays an evil nanny who manipulates the family of a young disabled girl she has been brought in to care for. The rather macabre role would have perhaps given many actors the opportunity to overplay the grotesque into caricature, but Diana was praised for her subtle yet creepy performance. She was occasionally offered film roles, but appearances in the little-remembered comedies *Bedtime with Rosie* (1974) and *Three for All* (1975) did not bring about the big-screen resurgence she hoped for. As the year turned to autumn, she celebrated her sixth wedding anniversary and spent time with Jason.

One evening in late 1974, after complaining of a terrible headache, Diana collapsed and was rushed to hospital. She was diagnosed with meningitis and was seriously ill, with doctors not sure she would pull through. Lake was beside himself with worry, but she was hanging on and within a few days, she started to recover. Her hospital room was awash with flowers and cards from well-wishers. She had visits from friends and received telephone calls from stars including Joan Crawford. Diana was touched by their affection. She thought herself indestructible, 'a bit of old Britain', and she assumed she would pull through. Luckily, she did, and without any long-term effects. After her recovery, Diana agreed to take a role in a tour of a play that Lake was starring in: *Murder Mistaken* by Janet Green. She thought it would be good for them to work together again after so long. But unfortunately, Lake's heavy drinking marred the experience greatly, making every performance stressful for her.

Still Diana's screen career was not gaining momentum. Throughout the 1970s, the British film industry was in decline. The artistic heights of the 1960s, with the British New Wave and its cultural impact, were a distant memory. Despite a number of high-quality films being made, the general output was weak. The early 1970s had seen films like Mike Hodges' *Get Carter* (1971), Ken Russell's *The Devils* (1971), and *Performance* (1970), directed by Donald Cammell and Nicolas Roeg, break new artistic ground and bolster British cinema's reputation for risk-taking. However, by halfway through the decade, most of the major American studios had closed down their UK operations, and the hugely crippling taxation being applied to the industry was driving the big talent out of Britain. Changes in viewing habits and in the structure of the film industry meant that by 1970, only two per cent of the population was visiting the cinema at least once a week or more, compared to around a third in the latter part of the 1940s.

As audiences declined, so did the investment in cinema infrastructure and in the cinemas themselves. This, in turn, put audiences off even more, as the comfort of the cinemas reduced due to the lack of care and the viewing experience declined. People continued to stay away. The breadth and quality of the films available to screen was also in decline, and production was down in other territories, including the US, so the availability of actual films to screen was suffering. This hit the smaller independent cinemas particularly hard.

The types of film available to screen narrowed as the industry changed and modernised. When film censorship was relaxed in the early 1970s, there was an increase in more explicit content being accepted and allowed to screen. This opened the doors to more alternative, low-budget genre films in niche subjects such as horror and exploitation cinema, but it also allowed for higher-profile films such as Stanley Kubrick's *A Clockwork Orange* (1971) and Sam Peckinpah's *Straw Dogs* (1971) to be allowed on screen. This raised concern amongst cultural commentators and moral campaigners alike. Screen choices were limited as films were not being produced or distributed to the same extent, and British film companies narrowed their scope. This led to a very different cinema landscape opening up throughout the decade in the UK.

Diana was still working in films sporadically, but like many of her contemporaries, the choice of roles she was offered ticked every box when it came to 1970s British film stereotypes; sleazy sex comedies, TV sitcom spin-offs and cheaply made horror films. Whilst in recent years there has been a revisiting of some of these film genres and a re-assessment of their cultural value, at the time, little credence was given to such output domestically and on the international stage. The cleverness of British cinema had given way to crassness, and every role felt like a compromise. Actors had such little choice. As Diana herself commented later on in 1977, 'I hate what is happening in British cinema today...I still get sent film scripts but I reject them with alarming regularity.'

A film genre that did succeed in 1970s Britain was horror – and Diana was very much a part of it. Horror was already an established part of the cinematic landscape, but the 1970s saw it diversify. The impact of cultural change and the reduction in censorship meant an increase of sex and exploitation elements entering the horror genre. The sensationalism of the British sex film heavily influenced the move to explicit content and a bid to capture an audience at a time of general industry decline. European horror cinema and its use of similar explicit violence and sexual scenes were also an influence. Stronger elements of brutality and terror appeared, often through foreign influences such as the US market and the success of films like *The Texas Chainsaw Massacre* (1974). It certainly secured box office results. As the decade progressed, horror films became bigger in their scope, with input from Europe, particularly Germany, and the impact of big American blockbuster successes such as *The Omen* in 1976. Horror largely fell into distinct sub-genres as a result. As horror director Peter Sasdy commented, audiences tended to split into three groups, 'One: the large number of people who go to the films to be frightened; Two: those who go for a certain kind of laugh; and Three: the type of audience that goes for sexual thrills.'

Diana's career certainly benefited from the peak of the British horror film in the early part of the decade. Between 1973 and 1974, she appeared in several films in the genre. Her first, *Nothing but the Night* (1973), was directed by Peter Sasdy and stars horror stalwarts, Christopher Lee and Peter Cushing. After the mysterious deaths of several trustees of a foundation that looks after orphaned children on a remote Scottish island, police officer Colonel Bingham (Lee) investigates with the help of psychiatrist Sir Mark Ashley, played by Cushing. Diana stars as Anna Harb, the wayward mother of one of the children, Mary, played by a young Gwyneth Strong in an excellent performance. Harb has a history of mental illness and prostitution, but she is determined to be reunited with her child, who was taken away from her and sent to the orphanage. Diana's character is full of mystery and intrigue, and we are never sure of her motives. But even with her wild red hair and provocative clothing, Diana is unmistakable in the role and gives a rousing performance, making the most of what is a largely underdeveloped character.

Diana also appeared in *Theatre of Blood* (1973), a horror comedy about an actor taking revenge on the theatre critics who ruined his career, starring Vincent Price and Diana Rigg. Other roles included *From Beyond the Grave* (1974), the last in a seven-part series of horror anthologies comprising several acts made by Amicus, a key studio in British horror productions of the 1960s and 1970s. Diana stars in Act Two of the anthology, *An Act of Kindness*, with Donald Pleasence and Ian Bannen as a frustrated middle-aged man stuck in a loveless marriage with Diana's character. She also appeared in *Craze* (1974) with Jack Palance, directed by Freddie Francis who made a number of horror films in the 1960s and 1970s. Francis was also a respected cinematographer, working on *Room at the Top* (1959), *Saturday Night and Sunday Morning* (1960), *Sons and Lovers* (1960) and

The Innocents (1961) in the 1960s; *The Elephant Man* with director David Lynch in 1980; and Martin Scorsese's remake of *Cape Fear* in 1991.

As with other British film genres, the decline in horror film production began in the mid-1970s. Between 1973 and 1974, the years in which Diana herself appeared in a number of films, thirty British horror films were produced. However, during the next four years, 1975 to 1978, there was a total of just twenty-two across the period. As a result, British horror film production became increasingly low-budget, independent and reliant on the opportunities for exploitation within the new video and home entertainment market of the dawning 1980s.

While the British film industry generally declined in the 1970s, the British horror film had bucked the trend and actually flourished in the first half of the decade, continuing to be a commercial success with a large number of productions. It was relatively cost-effective in terms of production, and repeatable, formulaic output led to continued success. Between 1971 and 1981, British horror films were the second biggest genre in terms of total productions in the period, the highest being children's films. British horror had some success in international markets, unusually for British films at the time.

By the end of the decade, however, horror was also feeling the effects of the stagnant British film industry and falling into decline. Even dominant industry stalwart Hammer Films was struggling, particularly to continue to break through into the lucrative American market, and the film studio collapsed in 1978. It marked the end of a successful era in British film-making.

Often the film scripts Diana was sent would require her to take her clothes off, but nudity on screen had never been something she had ever done. She had always acknowledged her sex symbol status, but said, 'We knew how to be daring without having to show too much.' While European and American film-makers ventured further with adult content, British sex films were largely bawdy comedies rooted in the era of Victorian saucy postcards and vaudeville. They were an extension of the nation's liking for silly innuendo as seen in the success of the *Carry On...* films. Like celluloid peep shows, softcore sex films were made for cheap laughs and titillation.

There had always been a strong tradition of British smut, and film-makers and distributors had always known the value of nudity. The rules of film censorship meant that any flesh on show had to be presented under the banner of science, education or perhaps documentary. As film journalist Matthew Sweet indicated in his book *Shepperton Babylon*, 'They searched energetically for contexts in which naked flesh would be acceptable to the censor, and produced travelogues exploring naturist clubs, documentaries in which men in white coats conducted grave discussions about sexual positions, full-frontal farces.' But whereas earlier forays into sexual content, such as *Naked – as Nature Intended* (1961), had navigated the rules imposed by the film censors with a creative flair for what they could get away with, content was becoming increasingly daring. 'Sexploitation' and cheaply made skin flicks, softcore porn that previously had only been available under the counter in a sex shop, was becoming increasingly lucrative and accessible. By the 1970s, the output was increasing and entering the mainstream, with various dodgy-titled films such as *I'm Not Feeling Myself Tonight* (1976) filling the void left by the absence of other studio output. *The Confessions Of...* series ran and ran, and *Come Play with Me* (1977) became the longest-running film in British film history. All forms of weak innuendo were exploited, turnover was quick, quality was low, and audiences barely batted an eyelid.

By the mid-seventies, Diana eventually found herself appearing in the *Adventures of...* series of films, which are often seen as a second-rate version of the *Confessions of...* films of the era, and that really is saying something. It was essentially cheaply made smut dressed up in flares and tight T-shirts, without the light comic touch of Robin Askwith to save it. Stanley Long's *Adventures of a Taxi Driver* (1976) saw her starring alongside Barry Evans and Judy Geeson. There were two follow-up films in the series: *Adventures of a Private Eye* (1977), which Diana also appeared in as the predictably titled Mrs Horne, and *Adventures of a Plumber's Mate* (1978).

Released in 1975, like the majority of British 1970s sex comedies, *Adventures of a Taxi Driver* was neither very funny nor very sexy. Yet it earned more at the box office than its similarly titled arthouse contemporary, Martin Scorsese's *Taxi Driver* released the same year. Diana also appeared in *The Amorous Milkman* (1975) which was written, produced and directed by Derren Nesbitt. Ironically, when photos purporting to be of her bare bottom being spanked on set were published in a porn magazine, Diana was outraged and threatened legal action. She had never done nudity herself and had no intention ever to do so. It was, it turned out, the bottom of another actress in the film. Writing about the film a few years later, David Parkinson in *The Radio Times* commented, 'The most significant thing about this bawdy trash is what it says about the state of the British film industry at the time – it's sad that this was the only worthwhile work Diana Dors, Roy Kinnear and other talented actors could find.' In the 1970s, sex comedies accounted for the majority of British film productions, so actors had little choice. Diana also starred in *Keep it Up Downstairs* (1976), which follows the adventures of the sex-crazed inhabitants of a bankrupt castle, and also starred Jack Wild and Willie Rushden. A hardcore version of the film was also released with body doubles replacing the leading actors. Diana also appeared in American / Swedish co-production *What the Swedish Butler Saw* in 1975, a sex comedy which was shot in Stereoscopic 3D and re-released during the 1980s 3D cinema revival.

Alan Lake also appeared in a handful of tawdry titles throughout the decade, including *The Playbirds* (1978) and *The Office Party* (1976). Lake and Diana appeared together in the 1979 film, *Confessions from the David Galaxy Affair*. Directed by prolific sex comedy director, Willy Roe, Lake starred as the eponymous David Galaxy, an astrologer and notorious playboy who finds himself a suspect in a robbery case and needs an alibi. Diana plays his landlady (again) and also sang the jaunty theme tune. The unfortunate cast included Derek Griffith, Tony Booth, Bernie Winters and Mary Millington. It had a tagline of 'Mary Millington meets Super-Stud!' and was produced by prolific Sexploitation financier and pornographer, David Sullivan. Millington was reportedly his lover at the time and starred in many of the sex comedy films produced during the decade. Sadly, in her later years, Millington struggled with depression. She also came under increasing pressure from the frequent police raids on her infamous Tooting sex shop for selling illegal materials. After a downward spiral of drug addiction, shoplifting and running up debts, she died aged 33 of an overdose of medication mixed with vodka.

The rather ironic situation of appearing in sex films together was not lost on Diana and Lake. Whether Diana agreed to be in the film just to keep an eye on her husband is disputed, with Diana herself commenting that it was just work and 'only a job'. Lake, perhaps, could not help but enjoy the experience of several naked women trying it on, but once the working day was over, he made a point of saying it was back home to 'the missus' for him. By the latter years of the decade, audiences had dried up for the peculiarly British but distinctly unerotic sexploitation films.

In 1975, aged 44, Diana discovered she was unexpectedly pregnant again. The news left her in turmoil. She felt she would be unable to cope with a young baby at her age and she was very concerned about Lake's drinking. But she put her fears aside and came to terms with the fact she was going to be a mother again. The news was made public and she told the writer Marjorie Proops that, 'This wonderful, unexpected pregnancy is the great gift of my tranquil middle age.' Sadly, during her eighth month of pregnancy, when Diana went for her usual check-up, the doctor expressed concern that he could not hear a heartbeat. Further examinations could not confirm whether she had lost the baby, and a short time later she went into labour. Their son was stillborn and although Diana never saw the baby, Lake told her he looked just like Jason.

After years of drinking, and perhaps finally acknowledging the pain and suffering that his behaviour was causing for Diana and their son Jason, who was now 6, Lake sought treatment for alcoholism. When he returned home, Diana experienced the peace and tranquillity she had craved for so long. He seemed to be a changed man. It did not last unfortunately, and he did relapse. It affected his health, including a collapse and a stay in hospital. Lake continued to go downhill, and even appeared in court charged with being drunk and disorderly. Diana felt their life was in tatters. She felt deeply ashamed of him and refused to be seen with him, even withdrawing from seeing friends. She, by her own admission, had become conditioned to life with an alcoholic. It was all-consuming and a trying time for Diana, yet she continued to work and to get through it.

She also had the constant disappointment and heartache of rarely seeing her older sons, who were still in America. Contact was minimal during that time, and she recalled that she would sometimes hear through friends that Dickie, or Richard as he was known professionally, had been speaking to the press about their failed relationship, and how he had apparently been jilted by her and left to cope alone with their boys. His professional success with *Hogan's Heroes* meant there was a lot of attention on him. Diana suggested in her own writing that Dawson prevented her sons from maintaining contact with her and, of course, gossip in the press did not help matters. He was an award-winning star in America, with shows such as *Family Feud*, and they had taken him to their hearts. Diana also claimed that a 'cold war raged between them' during the 1970s, and her account of the time and her apparently disjointed interactions with her sons in America were well-covered in her 1981 autobiography.

Whatever the situation, it was obviously a great source of frustration and upset for Diana that she did not have all of her children in her life in the way she wanted. Contact was sporadic for many years. Her account of a particularly difficult trip to see them after a very long time was heart-breaking, as she recalls the strained relationships and the feeling of saying goodbye again, 'Eventually the dreaded moment came for me to leave them again. It was the story of our lives – a wonderful time together and then the inevitable parting.'

In the winter of 1975, a few months after Diana and Lake lost their baby son, they took a trip to America with Jason. Mark and Gary had not seen their younger brother for six years. Diana recalled the moment she saw them at the airport, two grown-up young men of 16 and 14. She felt the trip to be a successful one this time, pleased to have her family all around her. But the distance between them was huge; the boys had no wish to visit the UK, it seemed, and Diana was not able to move to California to be nearer to them. The years passed by with sporadic contact, and relations remained complex. Once they grew older and became independent, it seems they were able to maintain contact themselves, without the added layers of fatherly protection, perhaps. But they also had their own lives to lead, like any young adults, so the relationship still ebbed and flowed. At the age of just 19, Diana's eldest son Mark married. She thought him too young, but he was the same age she had been when she married Dennis Hamilton. Diana did not attend the wedding. The rollercoaster relationship with her sons would continue to dominate her life for years to come, and after her death. Family ties can bind people together, but they can also tear them apart.

Whilst her film career floundered, Diana's television career thankfully continued to provide more substantial roles. She appeared as Mrs Bott in two series of *Just William* based on the very popular series of books by Richmal Crompton about an unruly schoolboy and his adventures. Made by London Weekend Television, it aired for two series between 1977 and 1978 on ITV. The thirty-minute episodes starred child actors Adrian Dannatt as William and Bonnie Langford as Violet. Mrs Bott and her husband (played by John Stratton) are a nouveau riche couple who spoil their fussy daughter, Violet Elizabeth. Mrs Bott is a social climber, eager to impress high-society people with her wealth, but she and her husband treat William and his friends with sympathy. Diana enjoyed herself, 'Mrs Bott is great fun to play…I can be as vulgar as I like.' As with her role in Lionel Jeffries' film *The Amazing Mr Blunden* earlier in the decade, the part gave Diana the opportunity to have fun with a character outside of the usual stereotyped roles that played on her sex appeal.

In 1978, she memorably played the 'fearsome' Lily Rix in an episode of the popular Thames Television police drama, *The Sweeney* entitled 'Messenger of the Gods' alongside John Thaw and Dennis Waterman. In the plot, a young lothario called Lukey Sparrow is accused of the theft of a valuable amount of mercury, but he has an alibi: he was in bed with a married woman. However, he needs to keep the matter quiet as he's due to marry Linda Rix the next day, and if the wedding doesn't go ahead, her formidable mother Lily, played by Diana, will hit the roof. Nothing will spoil her daughter's big day, certainly not the Flying Squad.

Diana appeared in the 1979 short film *The Plank*, made for Thames Television and broadcast on ITV. The slapstick comedy was written and directed by Eric Sykes and based on his own 1967 film of the same name. Although not a purely silent film, *The Plank* has no actual dialogue, just a series of grunts and incidental sound effects. It is punctuated by an orchestral score and a laughter track. Boasting an all-star ensemble cast including Sykes himself and Arthur Lowe, the film tells the simple story of two hapless builders who discover a floorboard is missing and try to navigate the replacement floorboard through the busy city streets, causing inevitable mayhem as they go. In a 'blink and you might miss it' appearance, Diana plays to type as an amorous woman in a bedroom window, suggesting Sykes might want to come up and join her.

The Plank won the coveted Rose d'Or prize at the 1980 Festival Rose d'Or in Montreux, Switzerland. It also proved to be rather popular in Sweden and was apparently broadcast regularly on national television over there until the 1990s.

Diana's television work continued into the early 1980s, with an appearance in an episode of ITV's *Hammer House of Horror* in 1980, and a guest role in West of England-based detective series, *Shoestring* starring Trevor Eve. In 1980, Diana delighted in playing a comedy role in an ongoing sketch within *The Two Ronnies*: *The Worm That Turned*. In the comedy spoof of dystopian fiction, it is 2012 and women rule England. Gender roles have been completely reversed, men are housekeepers and wear women's clothes, women are in all positions of power and are captains of industry. Law and order is managed by female guards, albeit dressed chauvinistically in PVC boots and hot pants. Big Ben has been renamed Big Brenda, the Tower of London is now called Barbara Castle and the Union Jack has been re-christened the Union Jill. Diana stars as the Commander of the State Police, 'A woman with an iron will, and underwear to match'. The Two Ronnies play the serial's heroes, Janet and Betty (men now have women's names and vice versa), who aim to flee this awful feminist state for the macho sanctuary of Wales. Diana obviously relished the role, playing the part with gusto and a twinkle in her eye. She was also given some of the best lines, wonderfully delivered with the comic timing she so rarely had the chance to demonstrate.

In early 1981, Diana had the opportunity to appear as Timandra in the Shakespeare play *Timon of Athens*, in an adaptation directed for the screen by Jonathan Miller and starring Jonathan Pryce as Timon. It was part of the ambitious and ground-breaking *BBC Television Shakespeare* series, which ran for seven seasons from 1978 until 1985, created by Cedric Messina and broadcast by BBC Television. By the end of its run, all thirty-seven Shakespeare plays had been adapted for the screen, and the series had proved both a ratings and financial success.

Messina was a BBC producer who specialised in productions of theatrical classics for the small screen. His ambitious plan to adapt all of Shakespeare's plays for television was viewed as an impossible task by many, but he persevered, and the *BBC Television Shakespeare* series was the most ambitious engagement with Shakespeare ever undertaken for the screen. Despite a daunting scope that frightened many corporation executives, its ambitious scale was championed as part of its appeal. As writer Susan Willis reflected, 'It was a grand project, no one else could do it, no one else would do it, but it ought to be done.' The project was so big that the BBC was not able to finance it alone and engaged with a North American partner, which would also guarantee access to the lucrative United States market.

Messina's concept for the series was to bring realism, especially in terms of the sets, and engage audiences who might not necessarily be familiar with Shakespeare or attending the theatre. Initially, the adaptations were quite cautious artistically and the first reviews were not brilliant. But once directors were afforded more artistic freedom and the interpretations became more daring, the critical view of the series improved. Several episodes are now held in very high esteem, particularly some of the lesser-known and less frequently staged plays, such as *Timon of Athens*, which Diana appeared in. The casting was impeccable too with many notable performances. It left an impressive legacy and at the time, it was apparently the only series whose sales completely covered the cost of making it, due mainly to worldwide sales.

While Diana found solace in smaller television roles, Lake's drinking ebbed and flowed. He sought treatment in 1976 and was sober for a few months. But the illness of his mother that year understandably caused a relapse. He was in and out of trouble as often as he was in and out of the local pubs. It felt like he was always looking for confrontation, apparently goading other men for an argument or a fight. Lake referred to himself in retrospect as 'roaring round like an eighteenth-century pirate...out of control'. He also put on weight due to the drink.

When Diana's son Gary came over to stay with them in early 1979, his arrival did not act as a catalyst for any change in Lake's behaviour. Sobriety was not achieved; it was avoided even more. A drunken escapade in Blackpool with Gary and 9-year-old Jason in tow made unfavourable headlines, and yet another fine for possession of an offensive weapon. Lake apparently threatened nightclub bouncers with a knife after they refused him entry. He was spiralling again. It might be coincidental perhaps, but during his stay in 1979, Gary also got into trouble with the police. Aged just 17, he appeared before magistrates in Chertsey, charged with driving recklessly, without a licence or insurance, and failing to stop after an accident. The accident was clipping another car and hitting a telegraph pole. Nobody was hurt, but he attempted to drive away and a passer-by spotted him. Despite Diana's pleas for leniency due to her claims of not realising that his American driving licence was invalid in the UK, Gary was fined and banned for three months. Even Lake was charged in the case for aiding and abetting the youngster.

Gary certainly kept himself busy during his time in the UK and, in a bid for pop stardom, he released a single. With the help of now-disgraced PR guru Max Clifford, Diana set about wheeling out the publicity machine. This time, it was in the shape of a horse ridden by Gary, which she walked through the streets while giving out copies of the single to bemused onlookers.

After the death of his mother from cancer in early 1980, Lake reached breaking-point. No longer feeling safe with his drunken and angry behaviour, Diana apparently left him, taking Jason with her to stay with friends. It was the jolt that Lake needed and as he begged her to return to him, he agreed to enter rehab. He said he would never drink again. But Diana had heard that before – why should this time be any different?

Chapter 11

A Time for Reflection

As Diana entered a new decade, she longed for an upturn in her career fortunes. Despite a lack of credible acting roles being offered to her, she had become a regular on television with numerous appearances in the late 1970s and early 1980s on game shows such as *Blankety Blank*, *Jokers Wild* and *Celebrity Squares*, hosted by her old friend Bob Monkhouse. Of the latter show, she once joked, 'God knows how they cram me into my little box.'

Diana had been a stalwart of the chat show sofa for a number of years, appearing on numerous shows, including famously with hosts Michael Parkinson and Russell Harty. Her intelligent and witty way with words, and a long and detailed memory for entertaining showbiz anecdotes, made her a natural choice of guest and she was always popular with audiences. One particularly entertaining appearance on *Parkinson* in 1971 was alongside her childhood sweetheart Desmond Morris, now a successful writer, broadcaster and painter. Kenneth Williams also appeared on the show. So popular was Diana as a guest on Russell Harty's chat show that, in the early 1980s, an entire episode was broadcast from the poolside of her home in Sunningdale. Other guests on that occasion included pop singer Adam Ant.

A long-held wish to front her own chat show finally came true in 1980 when Diana was offered her own discussion programme. After a successful pilot with guests Mary Whitehouse and comedian Judy Carne, *Open Dors* was commissioned for seven shows in the Southern Television region. Despite now being in competition with the big names like Parkinson and Harty, Diana was confident in her unique ability to draw out something different from her guests. She felt her showbusiness background gave her an advantage, as those in the industry like her, 'Hold a mirror to life…we are interested in others. We observe. We study. We understand.' Diana had certainly been observing the behaviours of other stars for many years, often at her own parties. She notoriously did not often drink or do drugs, but stood back and watched others at play. Those who worked with her and knew her have attested to her perceptiveness and rather long memory.

Never one to be bland, her choice of guests for her show were a fascinating and eclectic bunch. The first show of the series included Wolf Mankowitz and Lord Salisbury. She had Lord Montagu and Willie Hamilton, a notoriously anti-royalist MP, discussing the future of the monarchy on one show. On another, she hosted a fascinating discussion on pornography between Lord Longford, the politician, social reformer and long-time campaigner against it, and Paul Raymond, the notorious strip club owner and pornography publisher who was dubbed the 'King of Soho'.

The short series was well-received, and led to a six-part ITV lunchtime discussion show called *The Diana Dors Show*. Each week had a different theme, from fortune-telling to the question of what turns women on. Never one to shy away from a challenging conversation, Diana had always been fascinated by just how much people were prepared to reveal about themselves in public.

She decided to reveal a little more about herself too with the release of her autobiography, *Dors by Diana* in 1981. Diana also celebrated her fiftieth birthday that year, treating it as a milestone rather than a millstone around her neck. She had never been one to lie about her age, and at the party held for her by her publishers, she greeted questions about how she was feeling with honesty. After thirty-five years in showbusiness, she was still there and still relevant.

Her cultural resonance had been celebrated earlier that year with a cameo appearance as a fairy godmother in Adam Ant's music video for his 1981 number one hit, 'Prince Charming'. She appeared to revel in the opportunity to dispense kitsch magic with a wave of her glittery wand. That sort of cultural cache for a new generation would be repeated even after her death, for example, with her image appearing on the cover of The Smiths' *Singles* compilation album in 1995 in a still from *Yield to the Night*. Singer Morrissey chose her as an example of a post-war misfit, who moved on from suburbia to stardom but displayed tangible humanity by navigating several pitfalls. As writer Melanie Williams suggests, 'The disappointment and lost causes are part of the myth.'

Her fiftieth birthday bash went on long into the night. Diana still loved a good party, and she and Lake continued to host them at Orchard Manor. She was ever the consummate hostess; friends recall that she loved to entertain and be the one making sure everyone was enjoying themselves, even if the fun and frolics were often on the saucy side. She was still turning a blind eye to friends' antics, preferring to offer up more canapés rather than join in the fun herself. But she loved being there. As one friend recalls, she was always high on life.

As the year ended, Diana was in a reflective mood. She gave an interview to Clive Limpkin of *The Sunday Times*, in which she talked about the cultural and economic changes the country was facing in the 1980s. She reflected back on her impact in the 1950s as a girl who came from nowhere to become 'Britain's answer to Marilyn Monroe', with an enviably glamorous lifestyle. Acknowledging that it was largely fake, she said that the austerity of the times meant the public lapped it up. She felt that escapism was needed again in early 1980s Britain, 'They want a god and I'm their twentieth-century Boadicea.'

In 1982, Diana released a cover version of the Peggy Lee track, 'Where Did They Go?' as a duet with her aspiring pop star son, Gary. It was produced by Simon Napier-Bell, who was reportedly a massive fan of Diana's, describing her as 'a combination of Boadicea and Liberace. She is Britannia herself'. Napier-Bell even tried to stage a musical based on her life, with Diana as her own narrator. Napier-Bell had been a songwriter himself, with songs including the co-written 'You Don't Have to Say You Love Me' for Dusty Springfield, her only UK number one. He went on to work as a manager for Wham! Sadly, the extravagant stage musical of Diana's life never happened. That year, she also appeared on *This is Your Life* for a second time, almost thirty years since her first appearance on the show. This time, Eamonn Andrews introduced her by saying she had had 'a life that's had more cliffhanging moments than the plot of any movie'.

In the summer, Gary flew back to America again, frustrated perhaps with his singing career. Diana was upset but understood his decision. Her contact with her eldest son, Mark was non-existent, so the time spent with Gary that year must have felt so precious to her. She kept working hard. With Lake's lack of TV and film work, it must have felt like she was the only one keeping their heads above water. On 24 June 1982, after a hectic day as guest of honour to open a hotel, Diana collapsed at home with acute stomach pain. She was rushed to the privately-run Princess Margaret Hospital in Windsor, where she was operated on. Surgeons removed an ovarian cyst and performed a hysterectomy. After the operation, doctors explained to a concerned Lake that cancerous tissue had been removed during the procedure. Lake put on a brave face and reassured the waiting press that Diana would be back working in no time. Diana was devasted by the news when the specialist told her. Diana Dors could not have cancer.

She immediately cleared her work diary and took a few months off. Everything could wait, including the filming of *Yellowbeard*, Graham Chapman's pirate romp, which she had been scheduled to commence imminently. There was also another film role in development: producer Don Boyd was working on a story of the Kray twins and wanted Diana to play their mother Violet. She was very tempted as she had stated her admiration of Violet Kray previously, and her interest in the Krays had also led previously to a visit to meet Reggie Kray in prison.

Instead, Diana started treatment which included chemotherapy. But by early 1983, she was back working. That summer, she joined the team at TV-am. Producer at the time Greg Dyke had invited her to host a slot that morphed into 'Diet with Diana Dors', which ran every Friday. In typical Diana business-style, she apparently demanded to be paid in cash each week. She took part in a televised weigh-in to start things off, so that her progress could be measured each week. The target was for her to lose 52lb by her fifty-second birthday.

Weight had become an issue for Diana, once commenting that 'contentment ruins your figure'. The constant media scrutiny of her changing image did not help, something that had been in evidence since she first became a mother in the 1960s. Always proud of her figure, time had started to take its toll and she was unhappy with her bigger size. She did not like being called 'plump' and 'buxom' and hated wearing 'kaftans that hide a multitude of sins' rather than the flattering, figure-hugging outfits she preferred. But viewers identified with her struggle with losing weight, and with her 'dieting dozen', a group of viewers who were trying to slim alongside her, her segments on the show were said to reach the million viewers mark.

She seemed to enjoy her time on the show; she thrived in the relaxed atmosphere of the studio and it gave her an opportunity to shine, her effervescence and natural personality shining through the informal chats on the sofa. Her popularity is said to have helped the ailing TV-am to survive its early 1980s slump, along with the ubiquitous puppet Roland Rat.

Acting, perhaps, was not her main interest at that time, and she commented that she had no great desire to become Britain's leading character actress. But she was still open to acting offers, and had been considering a role in a West End stage version of *Whatever Happened to Baby Jane?* with Noelle Gordon. But in early September 1983, she was back in the Princess Margaret Hospital. It was a year or so since her first admission and during a routine scan, the doctors found traces of cancerous tissue. They arranged to operate immediately. Her husband was away filming at the time, appearing in an episode of the American detective series, *Hart to Hart* with Robert Wagner and Stefanie Powers on location in Greece. He flew back immediately, despite Diana's pleas to the contrary. After eight days in hospital, she was home in time for her son Jason's fourteenth birthday.

She also returned to work on TV-am, having missed just one week's appearance on the sofa. Viewers and production staff alike apparently had no idea of the personal trauma she had been going through. On the 28 October 1983 edition of the show, she revealed she had apparently met her weight loss target of 52lb by her fifty-second birthday, but it has been said that she simply removed an item of heavy jewellery before each weigh-in. Despite her poor health, in an interview with Jean Rook, she claimed she would outlive everyone, 'But maybe this is a test to find out if old Dors, at the end, really does warrant eternal life.'

Unfortunately, her time at TV-am came to a premature end. After a battle over claims she was promoting diet tools for personal gain – in this case, a calculator – which she disputed, she was apparently fired just a few weeks before her contract was due to end. She left the show in February 1984 under a rather heavy cloud.

In the spring of 1984, Diana started work on *Steaming* (1985), a film adaptation of Nell Dunn's stage play of the same name. Directed by the veteran filmmaker Joseph Losey, who made the critically acclaimed films *The Servant* (1963) and *Accident* (1967) with Dirk Bogarde, it also stars Vanessa Redgrave and Sarah Miles. The film centres around a group of women who regularly meet in a Turkish bath house, and together fight to keep it open when it is faced with closure. It is a film about female relationships and identity, with honest and direct dialogue about women's hopes, fears and realities. The film has the intimate feel of the original stage play, with the action largely taking part in one location and being dialogue-driven. Diana plays Violet, the manager of the bath house, who provides a maternal shoulder for the women to cry on. Losey was by then in poor health and the film was the last to be directed by him, released in 1985 just a few months after his death.

During filming, Diana was told that her cancer had spread to her lymph glands. She apparently did not request any time off from filming or special treatment from the production crew. She just got on with it. On 28 April, just after filming concluded, Diana collapsed with stomach pains and was rushed to hospital. Her bowel was blocked and doctors operated, removing a large blockage from her intestine. Tests also showed that the cancer was now inoperable.

The doctors told her husband that she might have just a few weeks to live. Both now Catholics, they prayed together with a priest. It soon became clear, however, that Diana was not going to make it. Despite the pain and heartache, she wore her favourite nightgown and still sported her treasured gold necklace emblazoned with 'DORS'. It all happened so fast; friends phoned and sent cards when they found out and she was so very touched by their kindness, but she insisted on no visitors outside of Lake and their son Jason. 'This isn't the way it was rehearsed,' she apparently managed to joke with her husband. Sadly, that night she fell into a coma.

Diana Dors died at 9 pm on 4 May 1984. She was 52 years old. Her youngest son lost his mum at just 14 and Alan Lake lost the love of his life. Amidst the shock, Lake gave a statement to the press who had gathered waiting for news of the much-loved star. He said, 'I lost my wife and a soulmate. My teenage son lost a mother, and I think the world lost a legend.' Her obituary in *The Times* said, 'Stardom may have long since disappeared, but she was still, undeniably, a celebrity.' The woman who had seemed to be an unbeatable tour de force, to be invincible, Britain's twentieth-century Boadicea, was gone.

Diana's funeral took place a week later at her local Catholic church, the Church of the Sacred Heart. Befitting her star status, she was laid out in a gold lamé evening dress with matching cape. She also wore her precious gold 'DORS' necklace. The small local church was packed to the rafters with friends and celebrities, showing just how popular she was in showbusiness. Attendees included Barbara Windsor, Shirley Bassey and Danny La Rue. There were many floral tributes too, including from the Kray twins. Locals and fans alike gathered outside the church to pay their respects, with the service broadcast to them through speakers. There were the inevitable journalists and press photographers present, but they were allowed to stay for the service. Diana's understanding of the needs of publicity was perhaps reflected in that decision.

The beautiful service was complemented by some of her favourite music, including *Ave Maria* and *Amazing Grace*. Tributes and readings were delivered by actor Patrick Holt, who had appeared alongside Diana in her first film *The Shop at Sly Corner*, and her very good friend Lionel Jeffries. Even the Mayor of Swindon gave a short speech. Later, as Diana's coffin was lowered into the ground, Lake apparently took a single flower from one of the floral tributes and dropped it into her grave, whispering 'I love you,' as he did so. Sadly, missing from the funeral were her older sons, Mark and Gary, and her ex-husband, Richard Dawson. It is not clear why they did not attend, but both her sons sent a single red rose sprinkled with glitter.

Alan Lake was devastated by his wife's death. He remained in their family home, Diana's belongings an ever-present reminder of what he had lost. He said at the time, 'To me she isn't gone…I can feel her in every room in this house. And when that feeling gets unbearable I can't help talking to her inside my head. I say "You can't leave me yet. You've got to be here".'

Lake had taken steps to sell the family home. In her will, which had been filed in 1981 around the time of her fiftieth birthday, Diana had left money in trust for Jason and Gary, but nothing for her eldest son, Mark. The reasons for this change to her will have never been made clear, although her contact with Mark had been sporadic and troublesome for her at the time of making it. The rest of her estate had been left to Lake. Orchard Manor was an expensive place to run and Lake just did not have the means to keep it on.

As the autumn months swept in, so did more reminders of Diana. October would see what would have been her fifty-third birthday, and November their wedding anniversary. It was too much for Lake to bear, and friends became concerned for him and his wellbeing. On the morning of 10 October, Lake dropped Jason at the train station as normal. Jason was working as an actor, and was in rehearsals for a play at the Barbican in London. The family's housekeeper reportedly felt concerned by Lake's behaviour when he returned to the house and asked him if he was OK; he apparently responded that he was 'In more trouble than you will ever know.' Later that morning, he was called on the phone by the journalist Jean Rook who wanted some comment from him on the sale of Orchard Manor, but he politely declined her. At 1.45 pm on 10 October 1984, Lake shot himself. He was found by the housekeeper, Honor Webb, in Jason's bedroom. There was no suicide note found.

Young Jason's care officially passed to his brother Gary, who became his legal guardian under the terms stipulated in the wills of both Diana and Lake. The funeral took place a week later. Many of the guests had attended Diana's funeral at the same church in Sunningdale just a few months before. Jason Lake was just 15 years old, but many guests commented on his maturity in the face of such heart-breaking circumstances. Lake's inquest revealed that he had been living with manic depression for some time. Coping with the death of his wife possibly caused his illness to worsen. It is likely perhaps that Diana was aware of his condition, although this was never explicitly said by her. She certainly stood by him through the complexities of his battles with the bottle and his health. Their love was intense and ran deep for both of them. Alan Lake was buried in the plot right next to his beloved wife in Sunningdale Cemetery, and later a joint headstone was added which read, 'together forever'.

Chapter 12

A Very Public Life

After the death of Alan Lake, the press began an onslaught of salacious headlines and coverage of Diana and Lake's life together. The newspapers were full of spurious reports of their antics together and apart, with stories of various affairs and supposed scandalous accusations. They also delved into their past, raking up misdemeanours and airing them yet again. People connected to their lives had their say with various publications, with some accounts verging on the ridiculous, others plain sordid. The press also dwelt heavily on Diana's complex relationships with her sons, particularly with Mark, from whom she seemed to be estranged. The family washing was hung out to dry for all to see.

Diana had always known the value of a well-timed tale or two. She knew how to play the press at their own game, at times making use of her power to sell a story. Sometimes she had been in control of that, calling newspaper editors directly when in need of a bit of cash, according to some that knew her well. Other times she had seemingly fallen foul of the nation's taste for salacious gossip and a celebrity fall from grace. When people saw the name 'Dors' in the papers, they expected scandal. As Melanie Williams suggests, 'Diana Dors' reputation as a star, even in its formative years, was founded upon scandal and controversy.'

By 1960, she had already been up in court, had her finances questioned in parliament, her private life debated in public, been accused of obscenity, and all the while still busily making a multitude of film appearances. Yet she was barely out of her twenties. 'Was there ever a British girl quite like Diana?' was the question posed by *Picturegoer* magazine in 1955.

That relationship with publicity began early on in her career. Inevitably, people refer to the period when she was married to Dennis Hamilton as the turning point in her quest for headlines, but there was earlier evidence of her publicity-savvy maturity. Spotting the chance to enter a beauty pageant on holiday in her teens, for example, and knowing the value of all those public appearances during her time with the Rank Charm School.

She knew how to conduct herself from a young age too. As early as 1955, the writer Derek Hill remarked, 'Diana Dors, it is generally accepted, has her head firmly screwed on.' But she also knew that one of her greatest assets was her looks.

The entrance of Dennis Hamilton into her life caused a great shift in her focus. On the face of it, it has often been assumed that he wanted to control her image and her career decisions, and to create a brand around her. Media manipulation became his forte. Whilst Diana admitted that he was always full of ideas and stunts, she claimed afterwards that not every publicity call was Hamilton's idea. The famous mink bikini she wore at the Venice Film Festival was always thought to be driven by his wish to make the most of brand Dors, but Diana later claimed the bikini was her idea, knowing it would cause a stir. She became more than a sex symbol, she was a 'blonde glamour machine'. Hamilton chose to capitalise on the opulence and extravagant lifestyle she had apparently become accustomed to as the only true British film star, and pushed the boundaries of taste and vulgarity in some people's eyes. But it was largely a façade. It also led to trouble. For Hamilton, there was no such thing as bad publicity as far as brand Dors was concerned.

It did not always work in her favour, however. Diana's first trip to Hollywood in 1956 should have been the big break she wanted, to build on her success back home. At the time, the press was delighted to welcome her, with one American film magazine decreeing she would be 'with us for four pictures and possibly a lifetime.' But it turned into a disaster, and she returned home under a cloud of controversy and disappointment.

She understood how the press worked, sometimes courting stories herself, other times bearing the brunt of the harsher side of their need to titillate their readers or bring someone down, 'In my life I have received as much publicity as Errol Flynn…and my name and photograph have appeared in thousands of newspapers all over the world.' When talking about a particular tabloid journalist, Donald Zec, who wrote about her often and with some acidity, with articles labelling her a 'Blond Gold

Mine', and 'The Bosom of Bray', and writing the stories describing her opulent lifestyle in the late 1950s which caused the taxman to pay attention, she said she always found 'his style of writing hilarious, even when it was against myself…I have a great deal to thank you for, one way or another. I still respect your pen, whether it is dipped in sugar or spice.'

The press often focused on her appearance, but as she got older the focus changed from her sexy 'blonde bombshell' antics to her weight. One particularly scathing comment from Jean Rook in the mid-1970s suggested she was now 'larger than life' and 'ripely and plentifully overflowing', to which Diana sharply responded, 'What you mean is I'm beginning to look like some marvellous Hogarthian whore.' Others compared her to the Albert Hall, to battleships and other large structures. She certainly possessed the elements of a national monument, something she happily accepted later in her career, enjoying her new role as a quintessentially British institution, a 'Twentieth-century Boadicea', who the nation needed in order to get them through austere times. The country had lapped up her faux glamour in the 1950s, viewing her with possessive pride as an emblem of Britishness and finding comfort in her make-believe and promises of stardom, 'All those tiger skins and waterfalls, I knew it was fake but they lapped it up – austerity days, you see? Now we're going through a depression and they need Diana Dors again,' she said to *The Sunday Times* in 1981. She was a British institution, part of society's fabric. They even named a bingo call after her ('All the fours, Diana Dors').

Diana's trajectory is tied in many ways to the society that moulded and surrounded her. Social change in twentieth-century Britain can be seen through her journey to fame and back again, navigating profound changes in social structures and expectations from the post-war period to the increasing personal freedom and social mobility of the 1960s and 1970s. She cleverly adapted her image and shifted with the times, becoming what the nation needed, and what she needed was them. Despite her sexual allure and glamour, she always maintained a down to earth self-mockery that meant she was attainable and tangible. She was happy to reveal her flaws and vulnerability, often with good humour rather than self-pity. She always felt like she was one of us, that she was on our side.

But the focus on her mass appeal and image was perhaps at the expense of her acting career. Despite some great performances, she never seemed to achieve the career trajectory that her acting talent could have garnered. Instead she appeared in countless films as the token sexy distraction or femme fatale leading men astray, once wryly commenting that she mostly appeared in bedrooms, nightclubs or in prison. She was typecast and trapped in an endless line of corsets and low necklines, 'Being a sex symbol made me and killed me at the same time,' she once commented. She had a reputation, both on screen and off.

But Diana demonstrated a shrewd understanding at a young age of how she was in danger of being typecast as the flighty young thing, flitting in and out of films for light relief, and not being given the opportunity to make the most of her acting skills in meatier roles, particularly in her early career with Rank. Later, there were opportunities along the way, which she grabbed with both hands, but they never seemed to lead on to a sustained run of good luck required to really cement her reputation as an actress. She always found herself running aground again, faced with a choice between typecast roles as the femme fatale or silly good-time girl, rather than face no work at all. She could not afford to be too choosy, but it impacted on her reputation.

Only in her later career was Diana allowed to really act and given the opportunities to do so. When the pressure of feeling the need to rely on her looks relented with age, and she was allowed to feel comfortable in her skin, she took on interesting character roles. She found herself feeling comfortable in television, which gave a number of opportunities in her later career in the 1970s and early 1980s. She was also allowed to have fun, taking on interesting comedy projects and appearing on chat shows where she could just be herself. There were bumps in the road, even in her more relaxed later years. Her success on TV-am, for example, was tempered by her hasty exit and the potential for yet another court case.

Despite the ups and downs of her career and personal life, Diana appeared to know herself very well. She also stood back and observed others. She demonstrated a sense of humour in her writing, and her anecdotes were pierced with wit and insight.

After her death, her private life remained fascinating to the public and the press. Rumours about her supposed 'missing millions' and their location bubbled to the surface, with talk of her utilising complex codes to keep her money hidden in secret bank accounts and fool the taxman once and for all. Yet the money was never located and apparently remained unclaimed. Years later, a TV documentary, *Who Got Diana's Missing Millions?* (2013), was made about the mystery. If the accounts are anything to go by, Diana could add a talent for cryptology to her list of achievements.

The effects of a very public life were also felt by her family, and her children in particular. Her youngest son Jason, who lost both parents in quick succession as a teenager, had personal battles of his own with drink and drugs, which were reported in the press. He died in 2019 aged 50.

Diana's personal story has been replayed in the press over the years, often as a fall from grace, with interest in the tragedy still outweighing any focus on her career. She is seen as an image rather than a whole person, a snapshot of blonde hair and pouting lips. But in recent years, there has been interest in her legacy as a performer. Film academics have re-evaluated her acting career and the cultural impact it has had. Popular culture has continued to feature references to her image and work. *Yield to the Night*, in particular, has continued to interest new audiences.

Unlike many of her contemporaries, Diana's image lives on through popular culture. Different generations remember her fondly, from those who watched her 1950s films in cinemas at the time, to those who saw her face on television in guest spots on comedy sketch shows or in early 1980s music videos, and the younger fans who found her work through popular culture references. Her films are regularly shown on television channels devoted to classic cinema in the UK, which has garnered new audiences, and reminded those familiar with her work of her impressive back catalogue.

Even early on in her career, she had an artistic impact beyond film. In 1956, the painter Stanley Spencer met Diana at a cocktail party in Cookham, Berkshire and decided he wanted to paint her, apparently commenting that, 'Diana had a simple beauty. Her pouting lips are particularly pretty.' Sadly, the painting never materialised. She featured on the cover art of The Beatles' *Sgt. Pepper's Lonely Hearts Club Band* album in 1967, designed by pop artists Peter Blake and Jann Haworth. The front cover sees Diana included alongside a large group of diverse celebrities and well-known figures, all as waxwork figures, cardboard cut-outs and other representations, as a 'cultural topography of the decade'. Shortly after her death, The Kinks also paid tribute to her on the song 'Good Day', from their 1984 studio album *Word of Mouth*.

Diana was a complex character, and always self-reflective and honest in her opinions. She knew what people thought of her, 'I have been described as a gold-digger, a sex symbol and a tough businesswoman,' she reflected in her first autobiography written in 1960. It was the suggestion she was a gold-digger that annoyed her the most, always keen to point out that it was usually the men in her life that had profited from her success. Of the term sex symbol, she was more accepting, 'I can't deny that I have a body. I think I have a brain as well.' Friends have often commented on her quick wit and intelligence, as well as her charm. But she knew the value of her looks and the importance of maintaining an image. Apparently, one agent in the 1960s wanted to insure her legs alone to the value of £75,000, a fortune at the time. She saw her sexualised image as a commodity and was prepared for it all to be consumed. 'I might as well cash in on my sex now while I've got it. It can't last forever, can it?' she commented in 1956. Some in the media thought this admission of monetary worth shocking, others supported her mercantile attitude as refreshingly honest. She certainly made the most of her moment.

Diana was not afraid to ridicule herself and her media image of a sultry sexpot though. Once, when asked by a journalist what it meant to be a 'sex symbol', she replied laconically, 'Well to tell you the truth, when I first heard the name, I thought it was a musical instrument.'

She was always pleased that in addition to the inevitable attention she got from men, she had a lot of female fans. Writing in 1960, she commented, 'My mail shows that middle-aged housewives and spinsters adore me. They identify themselves with me. I symbolise all they think they have missed in life.' But friends also recall that she was always approached by women who wanted to spend time with her when she was out and about. If she was in a club, it was women who approached her table for a chat and she was happy to oblige.

Despite a reputation for taking on so many 'blonde troublemaker' roles, some of her films demonstrated female camaraderie and a sense of solidarity. In *Lady Godiva Rides Again*, for example, she happily helps her fellow contestant to win the beauty pageant in a role that could have easily been played with bitchiness and spite. The story in *Dance Hall* focuses almost completely on the experience and friendship of a group of young women. In *Steaming*, her final film, she plays a supportive mother figure to a group of women who need each other. *Yield to the Night*, perhaps her most famous film role, shows her character forming an unlikely bond with the female prison guards, who show solidarity and sympathy to her despite the circumstances. In many of her films, her character might cause a stir, but she always does the right thing in the end.

Diana's love life was complex. She once reflected, 'Men have always been a constant source of amazement to me, their behaviour patterns, infidelities, and general problems seem much greater than that of we women.' She talked at length in her later books and interviews about the disappointments they had brought her. She was not afraid to give frank opinions about the various men in her life, particularly when she was younger. Her first autobiography, written in 1960, has an entire chapter devoted to the men she dated, and the ones she turned down, 'During my twenty-eight tempestuous years I have had to put up with all types of men – both on the film set and off it,' she wrote. She also wrote extensively about men and their ways in her other books, including the rather candid *The A to Z of Men*. But her reflections on her own relationships and the bad decisions she made romantically were often less candid.

Money – the pursuit of it and the loss of it – was a theme which came to dominate her life. She accepted that in order to survive, she needed to diversify her career, taking on cabaret to bolster her finances and keep her working and in the public eye. Her act was well-received by audiences and critics alike. It often paid well, but it was not all glitz and glamour in big casinos and fashionable nightspots. Sometimes, the agony of trawling the smaller British club circuit dented her confidence and drained her emotionally. Some critics suggested that she was trading on her own celebrity a little too much, with one particularly harsh review in *The Times* in 1958 suggesting she and others like her would be 'overtaken by their own celebrity; whatever talent they had is progressively masked and stifled by the habit of maintaining the personality the public expect to see.' But Diana herself knew how to work an audience, and was well aware of the influence that capitalising on her celebrity could bring.

The salacious headlines and controversy seemed to dog her for years and bankruptcy hung over her like a cloud. Yet despite her protestations of being an unknowing witness to her own financial downfall in later years, she was apparently fully aware of what she could get away with despite the threat of bankruptcy. A technicality of her trial meant she was found guilty as Diana Dors, so according to one friend, she simply started writing cheques as Mrs Dawson, her married name at the time. When cash flow was a problem, she would often find a way to access money.

Diana lived her life through the glare of publicity, developing a personal brand and a planned trajectory to fame and fortune, but did not quite achieve it. That applied to her personal life too. She once said of herself, 'I am a dreamer and am continually hurt and surprised when people let me down, or when life does not turn out right in my candy-box world of living.'

Writing as early as 1960, she said, 'Looking back on my mad, wild life...I would not change one bit of it if I had to live it again. Life is what you make it and, personally, I have no regrets.'

She perhaps became a parody of herself, all shiny blonde hair and overt sauciness, displayed for the comfort and pleasure of others. But she was a chameleon who went from being 'Britain's number one bad girl' to a familiar and comforting staple of British prime-time television, adding a touch of kitsch glamour to our drab lives.

She had an understanding of what it took to be a good actress from a young age and demonstrated a mature attitude towards what she knew would be a difficult path. Writing later in her career, she said, 'To become an actress, and even more a star, is not easy for a woman; and as the years go by her reputation, box office drawing power, and more important, the wrinkles on her face begin to make life uneasy and insecure.' She knew that acting was a place of jealousy and backbiting, but that she needed to 'brave the world and its gigantic microscope'.

She showed a lot of respect for her fellow actresses, particularly Doris Day, Joan Crawford, Yvonne Mitchell and Bette Davis, whom she described as 'the greatest actress and screen personality in the world'. She respected their craft and the way they conducted themselves professionally. There were others she did not like and made no bones about saying so quite openly. She was a woman who spoke her mind, after all. But often there was a hidden backstory influencing that opinion, usually involving the men in her life. She was not always as complimentary about her male acting counterparts, however, suggesting they were like 'overgrown schoolboys playing at being men' and reflecting on their insincerity and egotism.

Yet despite her frustrations with the business side of it, she wanted to act, to continue to experience the unique feeling of being in the studio or on stage, interacting with the camera and the audience. She had a unique and instinctive understanding of what the camera wanted, and what audiences wanted to see or hear from her. She sometimes moved away, concentrating instead on cabaret and glitzy stage appearances, yet she kept coming back. Her screen career played out in waves. She took chances, particularly in the latter years of her career. She did not shy away from a challenge, and when offered an opportunity to be seen afresh, she took it with bravery other actors might not show.

Her ambitions for international fame were dented by bad luck and bad decisions, being in the wrong place or with the wrong man. She had a tumultuous private life, enduring personal disappointments and tragedies, illness and pain, yet continued to rise phoenix-like again and again. Her bravado and determination perhaps fuelled her. Yet despite her life being lived under the constant glare of publicity and prying eyes, there are many aspects of Diana's life that still remain a mystery, even with her apparent openness. Diana Dors still remains somewhat of an enigma, just like a true film star should.

Appendix I

Filmography

The Shop at Sly Corner (1946)
Studio: George King Productions
Director: George King
Cast: Oskar Homolka, Derek Farr, Muriel Pavlow, Kenneth Griffith
Diana has a small role as Mildred. The film is also known as *Code of Scotland Yard*.

Holiday Camp (1947)
Studio: Gainsborough Pictures
Director: Ken Annakin
Cast: Flora Robson, Jack Warner, Kathleen Harrison
Diana has a small role as a jitterbug dancer.

Dancing with Crime (1947)
Studio: Coronet Films
Director: John Paddy Carstairs
Cast: Richard Attenborough, Sheila Sim, Garry Marsh, Bill Owens
Diana has a small role as Annette.

Good-Time Girl (1948)
Studio: Rank
Director: David MacDonald
Cast: Jean Kent, Dennis Price, Herbert Lom, Flora Robson
Diana has a small role as Lyla Lawrence.

Streets Paved with Water (1947) (not completed)
Studio: Gainsborough Pictures
Director: Joe Mendoza, Anthony Skene
Cast: Maxwell Reed, Jane Hylton, Andrew Crawford, Diana Dors
Production was abandoned.

My Sister and I (1948)
Studio: Rank
Director: Harold Huth
Cast: Sally Ann Howes, Dermot Walsh, Martita Hunt, Barbara Mullen
Diana has a small role, credited as 'Dreary Girl'.

Penny and the Pownall Case (1948)
Studio: Rank
Director: Harry 'Slim' Hand
Cast: Ralph Michael, Peggy Evans, Christopher Lee, Diana Dors
Diana plays Molly James.

Oliver Twist (1948)
Studio: Cineguild
Director: David Lean
Cast: John Howard Davies, Alec Guinness, Robert Newton, Kay Walsh
Diana has a small role as Charlotte.

The Calendar (1948)
Studio: Rank
Director: Arthur Crabtree
Cast: Greta Gynt, John McCallum, Raymond Lovell, Sonia Holm
Diana has a small role as Hawkins.

Here Come the Huggetts (1948)
Studio: Rank
Director: Ken Annakin
Cast: Jack Warner, Kathleen Harrison, Jane Hylton, Petula Clark, Susan Shaw
Diana appears as Diana Hopkins.

Vote for Huggett (1949)
Studio: Rank
Director: Ken Annakin
Cast: Jack Warner, Kathleen Harrison, Jane Hylton, Petula Clark, Susan Shaw
Diana appears as Diana Gowan.

It's Not Cricket (1949)
Studio: Rank
Director: Roy Rich, Alfred Roome
Cast: Basil Radford, Naunton Wayne, Susan Shaw, Alan Wheatley
Diana appears in a small role as 'Blonde'.

A Boy, a Girl and a Bike (1949)
Studio: Rank
Director: Ralph Smart
Cast: John McCallum, Honor Blackman, Patrick Holt, Diana Dors
Diana plays Ada Foster.

Diamond City (1949)
Studio: Rank
Director: David MacDonald
Cast: David Farrar, Honor Blackman, Diana Dors
Diana plays Dora Bracken.

Dance Hall (1950)
Studio: Rank
Director: Charles Crichton
Cast: Donald Houston, Bonar Colleano, Petula Clark
Diana plays Carole.

Worm's Eye View (1951)
Studio: Henry Halstead Productions
Director: Jack Raymond
Cast: Ronald Shiner, Garry Marsh, Diana Dors
Diana plays Thelma.

Lady Godiva Rides Again (1951)
Studio: London Film Productions
Director: Frank Launder
Cast: Dennis Price, John McCallum, Stanley Holloway, Pauline Stroud
Diana plays Dolores August. The film was known as *Bikini Baby* in the US.

The Last Page (1952)
Studio: Hammer Films
Director: Terence Fisher
Cast: George Brent, Marguerite Chapman, Raymond Huntley, Eleanor Summerfield
Diana appears as Ruby Bruce. The film was also known as *Man Bait* in the US.

My Wife's Lodger (1952)
Studio: David Dent Productions
Director: Maurice Elvey
Cast: Dominic Roche, Olive Sloane, Leslie Dwyer, Diana Dors
Diana plays Eunice Higginbotham.

The Great Game (1953)
Studio: David Dent Productions
Director: Maurice Elvey
Cast: James Hayter, Thora Hird, John Laurie, Diana Dors
Diana plays Lulu Smith.

The Saint's Return (1953)
Studio: Hammer Films
Director: Seymour Friedman
Cast: Louis Hayward, Naomi Chance, Sydney Tafley
Diana has a small role as 'The Blonde in Lennar's Apartment'. Known as *The Saint's Girl Friday* in the US.

Is Your Honeymoon Really Necessary? (1953)
Studio: David Dent Productions
Director: Maurice Elvey
Cast: David Tomlinson, Diana Dors, Bonar Colleano, Sid James
Diana plays Candy Markham.

It's a Grand Life (1953)
Studio: Mancunian Films
Director: John Blakeley
Cast: Frank Randle, Diana Dors, Dan Young, Michael Brennan
Diana plays Corporal Paula Clements.

The Weak and the Wicked (1954)
Studio: Marble Arch Productions
Director: J. Lee Thompson
Cast: Glynis Johns, Diana Dors, John Gregson, Olive Sloane
Diana plays Betty Brown.

As Long as They're Happy (1955)
Studio: Group Films
Director: J. Lee Thompson
Cast: Jack Buchanan, Janette Scott, Jeanie Carson
Diana has a cameo role as Pearl Delaney.

Miss Tulip Stays the Night (1955)
Studio: Jaywell Films
Director: Leslie Arliss
Cast: Diana Dors, Patrick Holt, Jack Hulbert, Cicely Courtneidge
Diana plays Kate Dax. Also known by the title *Dead by Morning*.

A Kid for Two Farthings (1955)
Studio: London Films
Director: Carol Reed
Cast: Celia Johnson, Diana Dors, David Kossoff, Joe Robinson
Diana plays Sonia.

Value for Money (1955)
Studio: Group Films
Director: Ken Annakin
Cast: John Gregson, Diana Dors, Susan Stephen, Derek Farr
Diana plays Ruthine West.

An Alligator Named Daisy (1955)
Studio: Rank
Director: J. Lee Thompson
Cast: Donald Sindon, Jeannie Carson, James Robertson Justice, Diana Dors
Diana plays Vanessa Colebrook.

Yield to the Night (1956)
Studio: Kenwood Productions
Director: J. Lee Thompson
Cast: Diana Dors, Yvonne Mitchell, Michael Craig, Olga Lindo
Diana plays Mary Hilton. Also known as *Blonde Sinner* in the US.

I Married a Woman (1956)
Studio: Gomalco Productions
Director: Hal Kanter
Cast: George Gobel, Diana Dors, Adolphe Menjou, Jessie Royce Landis
Diana plays Janice Blake Briggs. The film wasn't released until 1958.

The Unholy Wife (1957)
Studio: RKO / John Farrow Productions
Director: John Farrow
Cast: Diana Dors, Rod Steiger, Tom Tryon, Beulah Bondi
Diana plays Phyllis Hochen. Also known as *The Lady and the Prowler*.

The Long Haul (1957)
Studio: Marksman Productions
Director: Ken Hughes
Cast: Victor Mature, Diana Dors, Patrick Allen, Gene Anderson
Diana plays Lynn.

La Ragazza Del Palio (*The Love Specialist*) (1958)
Studio: Cite Films
Director: Luigi Zampa
Cast: Diana Dors, Vittorio Gassman, Franca Valeri, Bruce Cabot
Diana plays Diana Dixon.

Tread Softly Stranger (1958)
Studio: George Minter Productions
Director: Gordon Parry
Cast: Diana Dors, George Baker, Terence Morgan, Patrick Allen
Diana plays Calico.

Passport to Shame (1958)
Studio: United Co-Productions
Director: Alvin Rakoff
Cast: Diana Dors, Herbert Lom, Eddie Constantine, Odile Versois
Diana plays Vicki. Also known by the title *Room 43* in the US.

Scent of a Mystery (1960)
Studio: Mike Todd Jr Productions
Director: Jack Cardiff
Cast: Denholm Elliot, Peter Lorre, Elizabeth Taylor
Diana plays Winifred Jordan. Also known by the alternative title *Holiday in Spain*.

On the Double (1961)
Studio: Dena Productions
Director: Melville Shavelson
Cast: Danny Kaye, Dana Wynter, Wilfrid Hyde-White, Margaret Rutherford
Diana plays Sergeant Bridget Stanhope.

King of the Roaring Twenties: The Story of Arnold Rothstein (1961)
Studio: Bischoff-Diamond Films
Director: Joseph M. Newman
Cast: David Janssen, Dianne Foster, Mickey Rooney, Jack Carson
Diana plays Madge. Also known by the alternative title *The Big Bankroll*.

Mrs Gibbons' Boys (1962)
Studio: Halstead Productions
Director: Max Varnel
Cast: Kathleen Harrison, Lionel Jeffries, Diana Dors, John Le Mesurier
Diana plays Myra.

West 11 (1963)
Studio: Angel Productions
Director: Michael Winner
Cast: Alfred Lynch, Kathleen Breck, Eric Portman, Diana Dors
Diana plays Georgia.

Allez France! (1964)
Studio: CICC Productions
Director: Robert Dhéry, Pierre Tchernia
Cast: Robert Dhéry, Colette Brosset, Diana Dors, Ronald Fraser
Diana plays herself in a cameo role. Also known by the alternative title
The Counterfeit Constable.

The Sandwich Man (1966)
Studio: Titan International
Director: Robert Hartford-Davis
Cast: Michael Bentine, Norman Wisdom, Bernard Cribbins, Dora Bryan
Diana appears in a cameo role as 'First Billingsgate Lady'.

Berserk! (1967)
Studio: Herman Cohen Productions
Director: Jim O'Connolly
Cast: Joan Crawford, Ty Hardin, Diana Dors, Michael Gough
Diana plays Matilda. Also known by the alternative title *Circus of Blood*.

Danger Route (1967)
Studio: Amicus Productions
Director: Seth Holt
Cast: Richard Johnson, Carol Lynley, Barbara Bouchet, Sylvia Syms
Diana plays Rhoda Gooderich.

Hammerhead (1968)
Studio: Irving Allen Productions
Director: David Miller
Cast: Vince Edwards, Peter Vaughan, Judy Geeson, Diana Dors
Diana plays Kit.

Baby Love (1968)
Studio: Avton Films
Director: Alastair Reid
Cast: Ann Lynn, Keith Barron, Linda Hayden, Diana Dors
Diana plays Liz Thompson, appearing mainly in flashback with no dialogue.

There's a Girl in My Soup (1970)
Studio: Charter Film Productions
Director: Roy Boulting
Cast: Peter Sellers, Goldie Hawn, Tony Britton, Nicky Henson
Diana plays 'John's Wife'.

Deep End (1970)
Studio: Bavaria Atelier Films
Director: Jerzy Skolimowski
Cast: John Moulder-Brown, Jane Asher, Karl Michael Vogler, Christopher Sandford
Diana plays 'Mike's 1st Lady Client'.

Hannie Caulder (1971)
Studio: Cutwel Productions
Director: Burt Kennedy
Cast: Raquel Welch, Robert Culp, Ernest Borgnine, Christopher Lee
Diana plays 'The Madame'.

The Pied Piper (1972)
Studio: Sagittarius Productions
Director: Jacques Demy
Cast: Donovan Leitch, John Hurt, Diana Dors, Donald Pleasence
Diana plays Frau Poppendick.

Swedish Wildcats (1972)
Studio: Unicorn Enterprises
Director: Joseph W. Sarno
Cast: Diana Dors, Cia Lowgren, Solveig Andersson, Peder Kinberg
Diana plays Margareta. Also known by the alternative title *Every Afternoon*.

The Amazing Mr Blunden (1972)
Studio: Helmdale Films
Director: Lionel Jeffries
Cast: Laurence Naismith, Lynne Frederick, Garry Miller, Rosalyn Lander
Diana plays Mrs Wickens.

Steptoe & Son Ride Again (1973)
Studio: Associated London Films
Director: Peter Sykes
Cast: Wilfrid Brambell, Harry H. Corbett, Milo O'Shea, Neil McCarthy
Diana plays 'Woman in Flat'.

Theatre of Blood (1973)
Studio: Cinema Productions
Director: Douglas Hickox
Cast: Vincent Price, Diana Rigg, Ian Hendry, Coral Brown
Diana has a cameo role as Maisie Psaltery.

Nothing but the Night (1973)
Studio: Charlemagne Productions
Director: Peter Sasdy
Cast: Christopher Lee, Peter Cushing, Diana Dors, Georgia Brown
Diana plays Anna Harb.

From Beyond the Grave (1974)
Studio: Amicus Productions
Director: Kevin Connor
Cast: Ian Bannen, Ian Carmichael, Peter Cushing, Diana Dors
Diana plays Mabel Lowe.

The Amorous Milkman (1975)
Studio: Twickenham Films
Director: Derren Nesbitt
Cast: Julie Ege, Diana Dors, Brendan Price, Donna Reading
Diana plays Rita.

What the Swedish Butler Saw (1975)
Studio: Films AB Robur
Director: Vernon P. Becker
Cast: Ole Soltoft, Sue Longhurst, Charlie Elvegard, Malou Cartwright
Diana plays Madame Helena.

Bedtime with Rosie (1975)
Studio: London International films
Director: Wolf Rilla
Cast: Una Stubbs, Ivor Burgoyne, Diana Dors, Johnny Briggs
Diana plays Aunt Annie.

Three for All (1975)
Studio: Dejanus Films
Director: Martin Campbell
Cast: Adrienne Posta, Lesley North, Cheryll Hall, George Baker
Diana has a cameo role as Mrs Ball.

Adventures of a Taxi Driver (1976)
Studio: Salon Productions
Director: Stanley Long
Cast: Barry Evans, Adrienne Posta, Judy Geeson, Diana Dors
Diana plays Mrs North.

Keep it Up Downstairs (1976)
Studio: Pyramid Pictures
Director: Robert Young
Cast: Diana Dors, Jack Wild, William Rushton, Carmen Silvera
Diana plays Daisy Dureneck.

Adventures of a Private Eye (1977)
Studio: Salon Productions
Director: Stanley Long
Cast: Christopher Neil, Suzy Kendall, Harry H. Corbett, Diana Dors
Diana plays Mrs Horne.

Confessions from the David Galaxy Affair (1979)
Studio: Roldvale Productions
Director: Willy Roe
Cast: Alan Lake, Glynn Edwards, Anthony Booth, Diana Dors
Diana plays Jenny Stride.

Steaming (1985)
Studio: Worldfilm Series
Director: Joseph Losey
Cast: Vanessa Redgrave, Sarah Miles, Diana Dors, Patti Love
Diana plays Violet.

Appendix II

Selected Television Appearances

How Do You View? (1949–53)
Diana appears in various comedy sketches.

Armchair Theatre: **'The Innocent'** (1960)
Diana plays Jane Francis.

Alfred Hitchcock Presents: **'The Sorcerer's Apprentice'** (1962)
Diana plays Irene Sandini. The episode was not broadcast until several years later.

The Alfred Hitchcock Hour: **'Run for Doom'** (1963)
Diana plays Nickie Carol.

Armchair Theatre: **'A Nice Little Business'** (1964)
Diana plays Grace Maxwell.

Where Have All the Ghosts Gone? (1968)
Diana plays Megan Norton-Grey.

Queenie's Castle (1970–72)
Diana plays Queenie Shepherd in eighteen episodes.

A Taste of Honey (1971)
Diana plays Helen.

All Our Saturdays (1973)
Diana plays Di Dorkins in six episodes.

Thriller: '**Nurse Will Make It Better**' (1975)
Diana plays Bessy Morne.

Just William (1977–78)
Diana plays Mrs Bott.

The Sweeney: '**Messenger of the Gods**' (1978)
Diana plays Lily Rix.

Hammer House of Horror: '**Children of the Full Moon**' (1980)
Diana plays Mrs Ardoy.

The Two Ronnies: '**The Worm that Turned**' (1980)
Diana plays The Commander.

BBC Television Shakespeare: '**Timon of Athens**' (1981)
Diana plays Timandra.

Appendix III

Discography

Albums
'Swingin' Dors' (Pye, 1960)

Singles
'I Feel So Mmm' / 'A Kiss and a Cuddle' (Unknown label, 1954)
'April Heart' / 'Point of No Return' (Pye, 1960)
'So Little Time' / 'It's Too Late' (Fontana, 1964)
'Security' / 'Gary' (Polydor, 1966)
'Passing By' / 'It's a Small World' (EMI, 1977)
'Where Did They Go?' / 'It's You Again' (Nomis, 1982)

Bibliography

Braun, Eric, 'Diana Dors: In her own terms' (*Films and Filming*, February 1973)

Bret, David, *Diana Dors Hurricane in Mink* (JR Books, London, 2010)

Bryden, Ronald, 'The genius of Genet' (*The Observer*, 1 February 1970)

Conrich, I., 'The Divergence and Mutation of British Horror Cinema' in R. Shail (ed.), *Seventies British Cinema* (pp. 25–35). (British Film Institute, London, 2008). Retrieved 4 April 2020, from http://dx.doi.org/10.5040/9781838711528.ch-003

Crowther, Bosley, "Unholy Wife'; Diana Dors Stars in Movie at Mayfair' (*The New York Times*, 7 March 1958. Accessed 21 April 2020. https://www.nytimes.com/1958/03/07/archives/screen-unholy-wife-diana-dors-stars-in-movie-at-mayfair.html)

Davenport-Hines, Richard, *An English Affair* (William Collins, London, 2013)

Dors, Diana, *A- Z of Men* (Futura, London, 1984)

Dors, Diana, *Behind Closed Doors* (Star, London, 1979)

Dors, Diana, *Dors by Diana* (Futura, London, 1981)

Dors, Diana, *For Adults Only* (Star, London, 1978)

Dors, Diana, 'My Blonde Blunder' (*Daily Express*, 13 May 1959)

Dors, Diana, *Swingin' Dors* (WDL Books, London, 1960)

Dors, Diana, 'They Made Me a Good Time Girl' (*Picturegoer*, 7 October 1950)

Dors, Diana, 'Where I Went Wrong' (*Woman's Own*, 16 February 1974)

Gardner, Raymond, 'Powder blue bankrupt' (*The Guardian*, 10 February 1978)

Geraghty, Christine, *British Cinema in the Fifties* (Routledge, Abingdon, 2000)

Gilbey, Ryan, 'Deep End: pulled from the water' (*The Guardian*, 1 May 2011. Accessed 14 June 2020. https://www.theguardian.com/film/2011/may/01/deep-end)

Hall, John, *Dianamite yet* (*The Guardian*, 18 March 1970)

Hannan, Tony, 'Parting Shot' (*Forty20 Magazine*, August 2011)

Harper, Sue and Porter, Vincent, *British Cinema of the 1950s* (Oxford University Press, Oxford, 2003)

Hill, Derek, 'A window on Dors' (*Film and Filming*, April 1955)

Hinxman, Margaret, 'The Remarkable diary of Diana Dors' (*Picturegoer*, 7 May 1955)

Hirschhorn, Clive, 'I'm Out in the Cold Now, Says Diana Dors' (*Sunday Express*, 15 September 1966)

Limpkin, Clive, 'A Boadicea for the 20th Century' (*The Sunday Times*, 17 January 1982)

Macnab, Geoffrey, *J. Arthur Rank and the British Film Industry* (Routledge, London, 1993)

Macnab, Geoffrey, *Searching for Stars: Stardom and Screen Acting in British Cinema* (Cassell, London, 2000)

McFarlane, Brian, *An Autobiography of British Cinema* (Methuen Film, London, 1997)

Monkhouse, Bob, *Crying with Laughter* (Arrow Books, London, 1994)

Old Cranleighan Society, 'A High-Society Conman' (18 May 2016. Accessed 14 June 2020. https://www.ocsociety.org/2016/05/high-society-conman/)

Ottaway, Robert, *Picturegoer Film Annual* (Odhams Press, London, 1958)

Parkinson, David, 'The Amorous Milkman – review' (*Radio Times*. Accessed 21 April 2020. https://www.radiotimes.com/film/mt59n/the-amorous-milkman/)

Pix, 'Star from a charm school' (Pix, 5 August 1950, N.S.W: Associated Newspapers Limited). Web. Viewed 27 May 2020 http://nla.gov.au/nla.obj-468508659

Prall, Huw, *Passport to Fame* (The Book Guild, Kibworth, 2018)

Rook, Jean, 'Larger than life Diana – billowing into a new golden age' (*Daily Express*, 12 November 1976)

Rook, Jean, 'Diana Dors: The Great Survivor' (*Daily Express*, 29 September 1983)

Sloman, Tony, 'It's a Grand Life' (*Radio Times*. Accessed 14 June 2020. https://www.radiotimes.com/film/hvnx4/its-a-grand-life/)

Spira, Jon, 'When sitcoms go large' (*British Film Institute*, 6 December 2018. Accessed 14 June 2020. https://www.bfi.org.uk/news-opinion/news-bfi/features/great-british-cinematic-sitcom)

Stafford, Roy, 'A Boy, a Girl and a Bike' (*In the Picture*, 3 September 2011. Accessed 14 June 2020. https://itpworld.wordpress.com/2011/09/03/a-boy-a-girl-and-a-bike-uk-1949/)

Sweet, Matthew, *Shepperton Babylon* (Faber and Faber, London, 2005)

The Argus, 'Screen Review, New British Policy' (*The Argus*, 20 August 1949. Accessed 27 May 2020. http://nla.gov.au/nla.news-article22772889)

The Australian Women's Weekly, 'The indestructible Diana Dors' (*The Australian Women's Weekly*, 13 November 1974: 60A. Accessed 21 Apr 2020. http://nla.gov.au/nla.news-article51386541>)

The Australian Women's Weekly, 'The Three faces of Diana Dors' (*The Australian Women's Weekly*, 27 November 1963: 15. Accessed 12 May 2020. http://nla.gov.au/nla.news-article51193839)

The Courier-Mail, 'The Starry Way' (*The Courier-Mail*, 15 January 1949: 2. Accessed 13 May 2020. http://nla.gov.au/nla.news-article49927415)

The Mail, 'No Praise for Paulette in Drama' (*The Mail*, 30 August 1947: 3 (Sunday Magazine). Accessed 13 May 2020. http://nla.gov.au/nla.news-article55892164)

The Sunday Herald, 'They Left School' (*The Sunday Herald*, 7 January 1951: 5 (Features). Accessed 13 May 2020. http://nla.gov.au/nla.news-article18496882)

Upton, Julian, 'Carry On Sitcom: The British Sitcom Spin-off Film 1968-1980' (*Bright Lights Film Journal*, 1 January 2002. Accessed 14 June 2020. https://brightlightsfilm.com/carry-sitcom-british-sitcom-spin-film-1968-1980/#.Xp7bVshKg2x)

Variety, 'West 11' (*Variety*, 31 December 1962. Accessed 21 June 2020. https://variety.com/1962/film/reviews/west-11-1200420251/)

Williams, Melanie, 'Diana Dors: An angry young woman' (*The Independent*, 30 June 2006. Accessed 14 June 2020. https://www.independent.co.uk/arts-entertainment/films/features/diana-dors-an-angry-young-woman-6096758.html)

Williams, Melanie, *Female Stars of British Cinema* (Edinburgh University Press, Edinburgh, 2017)

Wise, Damon, *Come by Sunday* (Pan Books, London, 1999)

Worth, Jennifer, 'A Deadly Trade' (*The Guardian*, 6 January 2005. Accessed 14 May 2020. https://www.theguardian.com/film/2005/jan/06/health.healthandwellbeing)

Useful Resources:
https://www.dianadors.co.uk/
https://en.wikipedia.org/wiki/Diana_Dors
http://www.screenonline.org.uk

Index